lonely planet

Diving & Snorkeling

Bali & Lombok

Tim Rock

Susanna Hinderks

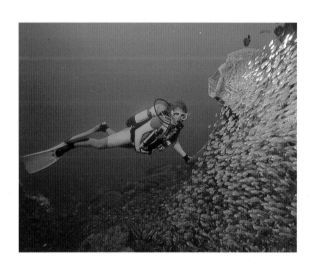

LONELY PLANET PUBLICATIONS
Melbourne • Oakland • London • Paris

Authors

Tim Rock

Tim attended the journalism program at the University of Nebraska Omaha and has worked as a photojournalist for 25 years. The majority of those years have been spent in the Western and Indo Pacific reporting on environmental and conservation issues. His television series *Aquaquest Micronesia* was an Ace Award finalist. He has also produced six documentaries on the history and undersea fauna of the region. He has won the prestigious award for Excellence in the Use of Photography from the Society of Publisher's in Asia, and has received many other awards for photography and writing. Tim publishes a magazine and works as a correspondent for numerous Pacific Rim magazines. He is the author of four other Lonely Planet Pisces diving and snorkeling guides, including *Palau, Guam & Yap, Papua New Guinea* and *Chuuk Lagoon, Pohnpei & Kosrae.* Lonely Planet Images and other agents worldwide represent Tim's photographic work.

Susanna Hinderks

Susanna is a native of Germany and has lived in and traveled in Asia for nearly a decade. A professional PADI scuba instructor trained in Thailand, she has worked in Bali for many years and travels extensively on ocean-related photographic expeditions. She is a studio photographer with an interest in nature and underwater photography, and she specializes in macrophotography. Susanna has assisted numerous internationally published photographers as a guide, field producer and model.

She often works with Tim Rock in the production of marine-related articles and translates the team's work for use in German and European publications. Her photographic work is represented by Lonely Planet Images.

From the Authors

Tim Rock I first dipped my head beneath Bali's seas in the early 1980s at Menjangan Island. Since then, the colors, diversity and sheer beauty of these reefs have beckoned me to return for many more pilgrimages. It is not only the undersea beauty but also the magnificence of the towering volcanoes, vast rice fields and exciting cities that makes this a dive destination like no other. I have watched the dive industry develop, prosper and mature since those early years. Now, international travelers can visit Bali and be assured of a world-class scuba experience.

I would like to thank the ever-cordial hospitality of Michael Cortenbach, Chris Brown, T.T. Yan, Takamasa Tanozuka, I. Bagus John Surjaya, Wirya and Puspita Santosa, as well as Wolfgang Daniel and Gede Suteja for assisting with dive terminology translation.

Susanna Hinderks I would like to thank Gary Bevan for being a patient and professional teacher, and Wally Siagian for sharing his passion and love for Bali's undersea treasures.

Thanks also to the people of Bali, whose gracious demeanor make this a fascinating and relaxing place to hang one's fins.

Photography Notes

Tim Rock's varied photographic equipment includes Nikonos II, III, IV and V cameras, Nikon cameras in Aquatica housings, and Nikonos RSAF cameras and lenses. He uses both Nikon and Ikelite strobes. Land cameras are the Nikon D1, F5, F100 and N90, used with Nikkor lenses. Hinderks uses a variety of Nikon equipment also.

Contributing Photographers Most of the photos in this book were taken by Tim Rock. Thanks also to Stefanie Brendl, Jimmy Hall, Bob Halstead, Susanna Hinderks, Sarah Hubbard and Tony Medcraft for their photo contributions.

From the Publisher

This first edition was published in Lonely Planet's U.S. office under direction from Roslyn Bullas, the Pisces Books publishing manager. Sarah Hubbard edited the book with invaluable contributions from Wendy Smith and Vivek Waglé. Emily Douglas designed the cover and book. Annette Olson, Sara Nelson and John Spelman created the maps under the supervision of Alex Guilbert. Lindsay Brown reviewed the Marine Life sections for scientific accuracy. Portions of the text were adapted from Lonely Planet's *Indonesia* and *Bali & Lombok*.

Pisces Pre-Dive Safety Guidelines

Before embarking on a scuba diving, skin diving or snorkeling trip, carefully consider the following to help ensure a safe and enjoyable experience:

- Possess a current diving certification card from a recognized scuba diving instructional agency (if scuba diving)
- Be sure you are healthy and feel comfortable diving
- Obtain reliable information about physical and environmental conditions at the dive site (e.g., from a reputable local dive operation)
- Be aware of local laws, regulations and etiquette about marine life and environment
- Dive at sites within your experience level; if possible, engage the services of a competent, professionally trained dive instructor or divemaster

Underwater conditions vary significantly from one region, or even site, to another. Seasonal changes can significantly alter site and dive conditions. These differences influence the way divers dress for a dive and what diving techniques they use.

There are special requirements for diving in any area, regardless of location. Before your dive, ask about environmental characteristics that can affect your diving and how trained local divers deal with these considerations.

Warning & Request

Things change—dive site conditions, regulations, topside information. Nothing stays the same for long. Your feedback on this book will be used to help update and improve the next edition. Excerpts from your correspondence may appear in *Planet Talk*, our quarterly newsletter, or *Comet*, our monthly email newsletter. Please let us know if you do not want your letter published or your name acknowledged.

Correspondence can be addressed to:
Lonely Planet Publications
Pisces Books
150 Linden Street
Oakland, CA 94607
email: pisces@lonelyplanet.com

Introduction

For many, Bali invokes images of picturesque rural towns set amid verdant tropical foliage beside an azure sea. For others, Balinese paradise is the surf breaking on the sandy shores of a bustling tourist town, where exotic souvenirs and an active nightlife are within a few steps of your accommodations. This tiny island in the middle of the huge Indonesian archipelago is all that and much more. Its rich culture, beautiful landscape and amazing marine environment attract visitors from around the world.

Lombok, Bali's eastern neighbor, has as much natural beauty as Bali, with tall volcanoes, sandy beaches and a varied landscape. It is much less developed but changing fast. For the time being there are few facilities for tourists. The Gili Islands, off Lombok's northwest coast, are an exception. Their varied accommodations and activities have made them a favorite destination.

Bali's vivid culture is perhaps its greatest attraction. Bali became a stronghold of Indonesia's elite Hindu society more than six centuries ago, when Islam spread throughout the rest of the archipelago. Hindu traditions are the foundation of

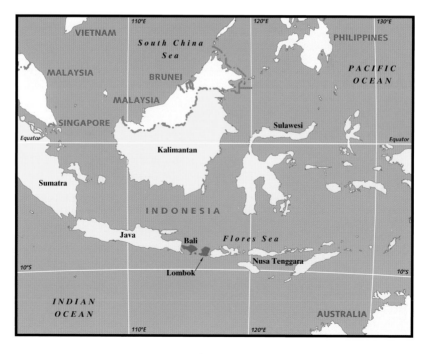

Balinese culture. When you drive down a road in Bali, you are likely to see colorfully dressed people on their way to a temple. Festivals, ceremonies, processions and dances are a regular part of life here and visitors are welcome to attend these celebrations. Traditional *barong* dances, plays and other theatrical manifestations of the culture are also performed for tourists.

The lush, fertile landscape supports the vast rice fields that enable Bali to be virtually self-sufficient. Locally grown fruits and vegetables make Bali's markets varied and bountiful. Volcanoes provide a dramatic backdrop to the fleets of colorful sailing and fishing vessels heading out to sea.

The Bali and Flores Seas, at the southern reaches of the Indian Ocean, surround Bali and Lombok. They support an incredible amount of marine life, making this one of the most biologically unique and diverse diving destinations in the world. Because of the plethora of land-based activities and attractions, diving sometimes gets overshadowed. But with abundant marine life, varied underwater topography and an established dive industry, the warm waters surrounding these islands can entertain both casual divers and dive-travel veterans.

Bali has a well-developed tourist industry and can provide services to please all tastes. Though political unrest has swept through much of Indonesia in the last few years, Bali has remained a safe haven, protected in large part by the desire to maintain the island's tourist economy. On Lombok's mainland, isolated incidents of violence have hindered tourism, but the Gili Islands continue to be a popular destination where access and amenities continue to improve. The islands' white sands, sapphire waters and underwater coral gardens won't disappoint.

This book describes 59 dive sites around Bali and Lombok, organized by geographic region. Detailed site information—including marine life, dive site depth range and recommended expertise level—will help you select the dives best suited to your interests and abilities. General information for each region can help you plan an enjoyable stay. The Marine Life section provides a gallery of Bali and Lombok's fish and invertebrate life. Though this book is not meant to be a stand-alone travel guide, the Overview and Practicalities sections offer useful information about the islands, while the Activities & Attractions section describes a few popular topside activities.

Bali's majestic Gunung Batur as seen from a Lembongan beach.

Full refund issued for new and unread books and unopened music within 30 days with a receipt from any Barnes & Noble store.

Store Credit issued for new and unread books and unopened music after 30 days or without a sales receipt. Credit issued at <u>lowest sale price</u>.

We gladly accept returns of new and unread books and unopened music from bn.com with a bn.com receipt for store credit at the bn.com price.

Full refund issued for new and unread books and unopened music within 30 days with a receipt from any Barnes & Noble store.

Store Credit issued for new and unread books and unopened music after 30 days or without a sales receipt. Credit issued at <u>lowest sale price</u>.

We gladly accept returns of new and unread books and unopened music from bn.com with a bn.com receipt for store credit at the bn.com price.

Full refund issued for new and unread books and unopened music within 30 days with a receipt from any Barnes & Noble store.

Store Credit issued for new and unread books and unopened music after 30

Overview

The island of Bali sits in the west-central part of the vast Indonesian archipelago. It has a land area of 5,620 sq km (2,190 sq miles). Boasting a growing population of about 3 million people, it is Indonesia's most popular tourist destination. The capital city of Denpasar, with its 400,000 inhabitants, is the economic hub of the island.

Bali's population is 95% ethnic Balinese. Likewise, 95% of the population is Hindu, with Muslims and Christians making up the remaining 5%. Balinese culture is influenced by a mix of Hindu, Buddhist and animist beliefs, which give rise to colorful dances and ornate religious festivals celebrating births, marriages, successful harvests, deaths and many other occasions.

The island of Lombok lies due east of Bali across Selat Lombok (Lombok Strait). Though somewhat larger than Bali, it is more arid and far less developed, sustaining a poor and mostly rural population of 2.4 million. The capital city, Mataram, is on Lombok's west coast. The majority of Lombok's inhabitants practice Islam and Wektu Telu religions. The latter is a combination of Balinese Hinduism, Islam and animism that originated in northern Lombok. The principle languages are Sasak and Bahasa Indonesia.

Though Lombok exists in Bali's shadow, it has all the scenic beauty of its more famous neighbor without the noise, the crowds and the increasingly touristy beaches. The small, coral-fringed Gili Islands are popular with travelers, who come by the thousands for the world-renowned diving and snorkeling. The Gili Islands' unspoiled quality is retained through careful development—a ban on paved roads, cars and other motor vehicles cuts down on the islands' noise and clutter.

History

Human fossils some 500,000 years old were found in east Java. Stone tools and earth-based pottery found in western Bali date back 250,000 years. Other finds show that the Bronze Age took place in Bali prior to 300 BC.

The earliest of the modern Indonesians came from India or Myanmar (Burma), though little is known of the period when Indian traders brought Hinduism to the island chain. Hindu influences spread to Bali during the reign of Javanese King Airlangga (1019-1042). The last important Hindu kingdom was the Majapahit, which was founded in the 13th century. The subsequent spread of Islam throughout the archipelago in the 14th century forced the Majapahits to retreat to Bali. This influx of artisans, musicians, actors, dancers and other creative people instigated unprecedented cultural growth and provided the foundation for modern Balinese culture.

Lombok's habitation dates back many centuries as well, but historical records about its development are scarce. The first recorded society is that of the Sasaks, 17th-century emigrants of India or Myanmar (Burma). They were farmers and practicers of animism, a religion than was markedly different than Bali's Hinduism.

The Balinese harmoniously ruled west Lombok from the 17th century until the late 1800s. A few Hindu temples stand as testament to Lombok's Balinese influence. Attempts to rule east Lombok were not as successful, resulting in a hostile relationship between the Sasak leaders and the appointed Balinese district heads.

By the 15th century, a strong but short-lived Muslim empire had developed in Indonesia, but the Portuguese overtook it in 1511. The Dutch displaced the Portuguese and began making inroads. By the early 20th century, the entire archipelago—including Aceh (Sumatra) and Bali—was under Dutch control.

Dancer in traditional Balinese costume.

Swelling nationalism, combined with Japanese occupation of the archipelago during WWII, served to weaken Dutch resolve. The Dutch finally transferred sovereignty to the new Indonesian republic in 1949. Achmed Soekarno, a proponent of self-rule since the early 1920s, became president. In 1957, after a rudderless period of parliamentary democracy, Soekarno overthrew the parliament, declared martial law and initiated a more authoritarian style of government, which he dubbed "guided democracy." Instability reigned for several years, during which Soekarno launched a "confrontation" against Malaysia, withdrew from the United Nations and planned to socialize the economy.

Events came to a head in 1965 when an attempted coup, allegedly by communist groups, killed several army generals and threatened Soekarno's hold on power. He repressed this coup and instigated a wholesale massacre of communists throughout Indonesia. On Bali, the result was particularly bloody, as a witch-hunt for "godless communists" led to mob scenes and brutal deaths. The military intervened, but not before an estimated 50,000 to 100,000 people (out of a population of 2 million) were murdered. Mass killings also took place on Lombok, targeted at communists, sympathizers and ethnic Chinese.

General Soeharto, who was responsible for brutally quashing the '65 coup, eventually seized presidential control. In stark contrast to the turbulent Soekarno years, Soeharto sought to address Indonesia's economic problems, forge national unity, promote openness and curb the country's worst excesses.

In 1997 and '98 Indonesia's economy took a dramatic downturn. By January 1998, 2.5 million people had lost their jobs and the International Monetary Fund was imposing austerity measures in return for sizable loans.

The president became increasingly out of touch with the mood of the nation. Food shortages and rising prices sparked antigovernment sentiments. Soeharto eventually stepped down in May 1998. His (none-too-popular) vice president, Jusuf Habibie, replaced him.

In November 1998, the brewing tensions again boiled over into mass rioting and a series of bloody confrontations throughout the archipelago—but Bali remained peaceful. Things cooled down for a short time, but heated up again in October 1999, when Mr. Abdurrahman Wahid, a moderate Islamic leader, was chosen as Indonesia's first democratically elected President over the populist candidate, Mrs. Megawati Soekarnoputri. Megawati supporters took to the streets armed with rocks and Molotov cocktails, riot police were called in, bombs exploded and the country returned to living precariously.

The Balinese have taken great pains to ensure that political strife, which seems to constantly plague Indonesia, has no effect on the island. A huge investment in the tourist industry has helped Bali grow economically, especially in the last two decades. Infrastructure—in the form of roads, telecommunications, utilities and accommodations—has been vastly improved. The island remains a stable and safe destination for tourists worldwide.

While Bali has been the golden child in this wave of development, Lombok has played the role of poor stepsister. Lombok has enjoyed stability and some growth, but nothing compared with the wealth of Bali. Though Lombok's esteem increased when the city of Mataram was named administrative capital of West Nusa Tenggara in 1958, crop failures and food shortages in 1966 and 1973 have been burdens. These problems, coupled with a decrease in tourism in the late 1990s due to political instability, have been economically disastrous. It may be several years before Lombok's tourism industry recovers fully.

Diving History

Diving in Bali started in earnest in the late 1960s and early 1970s, with hardy explorers packing tanks around the island to explore the points, outcrops and offshore reefs and islands. Word of

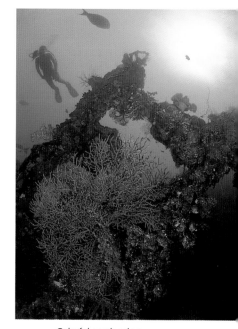

Colorful corals adorn
Tulamben's historic wreck.

Bali's incredible undersea biodiversity attracted marine biologists from all over the world. A small but faithful following of adventurous Australian and European divers bolstered the fledgling market as tourism grew during the 1970s and '80s.

In the early 1990s, sport diving grew more popular here. Consequently, a number of fly-by-night dive shops opened their doors with only dollars—not diver safety, quality or environmental concerns—in mind. Fortunately, these shops don't usually stay in business long (their reputation has a way of preceding them). The better operations have thrived by providing quality sale and rental equipment, trained and insured guides and clean air fills. These operators put together fascinating tours to the popular sites around the island. Their conscientious conservation and development efforts have broadened the horizons of the Bali diving scene.

The Lombok diving industry is only a decade old. Operators have been an integral part of establishing conservation practices and developing technical diving in the region.

Geography

Bali

Bali is an island in the west-central portion of the Indonesian archipelago, flanked by Java to the west and Lombok to the east. Though Bali is relatively small, its topography is varied due to ongoing volcanic activity.

Crater lakes such as Danau Batur lie amid Bali's high volcanic peaks.

The southern peninsula is an arid area with limestone cliffs rising steeply out of the ocean. A narrow spit connects it with mainland Bali, which stretches north, east and west into broad, extremely fertile, terraced rice paddies.

A series of volcanoes, which are revered by the Balinese, form the central mountain range. Here you can explore cool lake regions, forests, clove plantations and some sparsely populated villages. Gunung Agung, Bali's highest and most active volcano, rises to 3,142m (10,305ft) and the range itself averages 2,000m (6,560ft). Gunung Agung violently erupted in 1963, killing thousands of people and devastating the eastern end of Bali.

The entire northwestern hills region has been designated as Taman Nasional Bali Barat (West Bali National Park), a preservation and conservation area. These older mountains are still quite rugged, with scenic valleys and seemingly impassable jungle. Wildlife and rare birds abound here.

The Bali Sea to the north and the Indian Ocean to the south feed Bali's coastal areas. The current-swept straits also feed the sloping coral reefs. Bali's underwater features include Menjangan Island's sharp drop-offs and the northern coast's sandy bays. The eastern slopes are fed by the rich nutrients from Gunung Agung, and the central coast area has a rocky terrain covered with corals fed by upwellings from the straits. The Nusa Penida cliffs are breathtaking, and the large underwater boulders to the south create a unique environment.

Lombok

Lombok is 8° south of the equator and is drier than Bali. The south is the most fertile part of the island, with rice fields, rivers and large plains. The east is very dry and sparsely populated.

Lombok is less developed than Bali and has uncrowded beaches, a bigger volcano and a more varied landscape. Towering Gunung Rinjani, Indonesia's second-highest mountain, at 3,726m (12,220ft), can be seen from anywhere on the island. The volcano's large caldera is home to hot springs and to Segara Anak Lake, which has been dived by a few adventurous explorers based in Lombok's Gili Islands.

Bali & Lombok

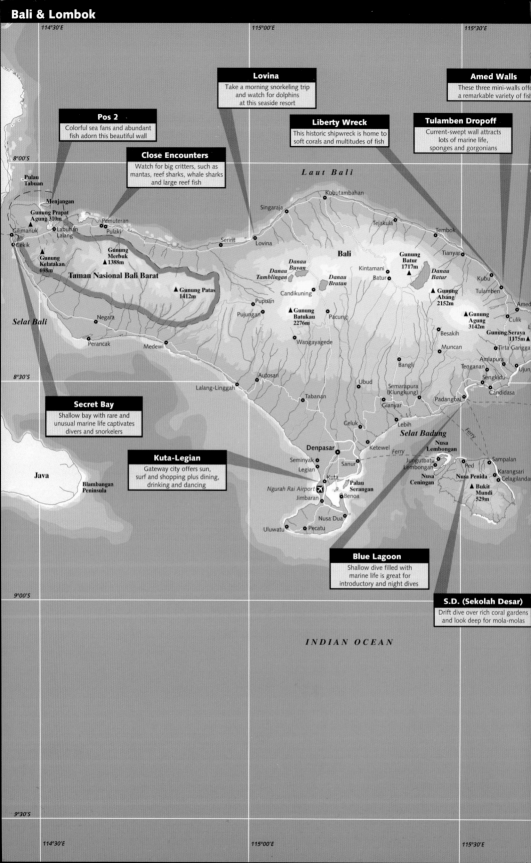

Pos 2
Colorful sea fans and abundant fish adorn this beautiful wall

Lovina
Take a morning snorkeling trip and watch for dolphins at this seaside resort

Amed Walls
These three mini-walls offer a remarkable variety of fish

Close Encounters
Watch for big critters, such as mantas, reef sharks, whale sharks and large reef fish

Liberty Wreck
This historic shipwreck is home to soft corals and multitudes of fish

Tulamben Dropoff
Current-swept wall attracts lots of marine life, sponges and gorgonians

Secret Bay
Shallow bay with rare and unusual marine life captivates divers and snorkelers

Kuta-Legian
Gateway city offers sun, surf and shopping plus dining, drinking and dancing

Blue Lagoon
Shallow dive filled with marine life is great for introductory and night dives

S.D. (Sekolah Desar)
Drift dive over rich coral gardens and look deep for mola-molas

8°00'S
8°30'S
9°00'S
9°30'S

114°30'E
115°00'E
115°30'E

Laut Bali

Bali

Selat Bali

Selat Badung

INDIAN OCEAN

Java

Kubutambahan
Singaraja
Tejakula
Tembok
Tianyar
Amed
Seririt
Lovina
Kintamani
Kubu
Tulamben
Pemuteran
Pulaki
Labuhan Lalang
Menjangan
Gilimanuk
Cekik
Pulau Tabuan
▲ Gunung Prapat Agung 310m
▲ Gunung Kelatakan 698m
Taman Nasional Bali Barat
▲ Gunung Merbuk 1388m
▲ Gunung Patas 1412m
Negara
Perancak
Medewi
Lalang-Linggah
Autosari
Pujungan
Pupuan
Candikuning
Danau Tamblingan
Danau Buyan
Danau Bratan
▲ Gunung Batukau 2276m
Wangayagede
Tabanan
Pacung
Batur
▲ Gunung Batur 1717m
Danau Batur
▲ Gunung Abang 2152m
Besakih
Muncan
▲ Gunung Agung 3142m
Culik
Gunung Seraya 1175m ▲
Tirta Gangga
Amlapura
Tenganan
Ujung
Sengkidu
Candidasa
Padangbai
Bangli
Semarapura (Klungkung)
Gianyar
Ubud
Celuk
Lebih
Ketewel
Sanur
Denpasar
Seminyak
Legian
Kuta
Ngurah Rai Airport ✈
Jimbaran
Benoa
Palau Serangan
Nusa Dua
Uluwatu
Pecatu
Blambangan Peninsula
Jungutbatu
Lembongan
Nusa Lembongan
Ped
Sampalan
Karangsari
Celagilandan
Nusa Ceningan
Nusa Penida
▲ Bukit Mundi 529m
Ferry

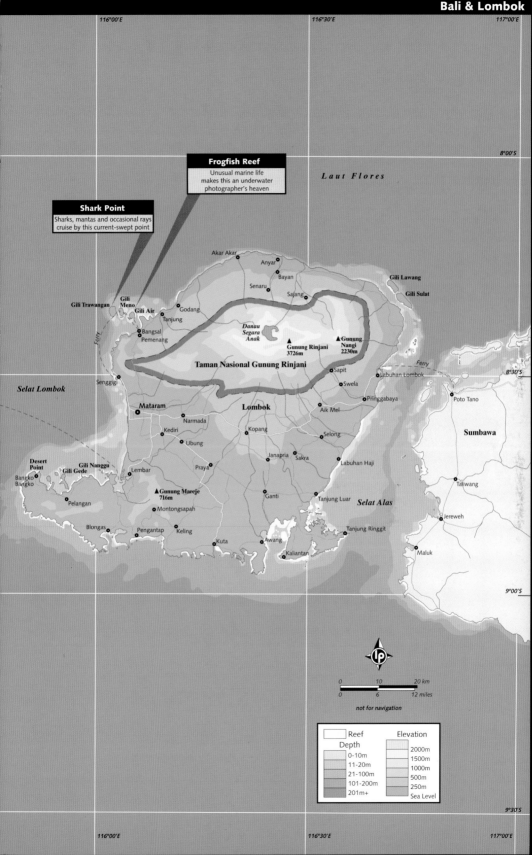

116°00'E 116°30'E 117°00'E

8°00'S

Laut Flores

Frogfish Reef
Unusual marine life
makes this an underwater
photographer's heaven

Shark Point
Sharks, mantas and occasional rays
cruise by this current-swept point

Akar Akar

Anyar

Bayan

Senaru

Sajang

Gili Lawang

Gili Sulat

Gili Trawangan

Gili Meno

Gili Air

Godang

Tanjung

Bangsal

Pemenang

*Danau
Segara
Anak*

▲
**Gunung Rinjani
3726m**

▲ **Gunung
Nangi
2230m**

Taman Nasional Gunung Rinjani

Sapit

Ferry

Labuhan Lombok

8°30'S

Selat Lombok

Senggigi

Swela

Pringgabaya

Poto Tano

Mataram

Narmada

Lombok

Aik Mel

Sumbawa

Kediri

Kopang

Selong

Ubung

Janapria

Sakra

Labuhan Haji

**Desert
Point**

Gili Nanggu
Gili Gede

Lembar

Praya

Taliwang

Bangko
Bangko

▲ **Gunung Mareje
716m**

Ganti

Tanjung Luar

Selat Alas

Pelangan

Montongsapah

Jereweh

Blongas

Pengantap

Keling

Kuta

Awang

Tanjung Ringgit

Maluk

Kaliantan

9°00'S

0   10   20 km

0   6   12 miles

not for navigation

Reef   Elevation
Depth
0-10m   2000m
11-20m   1500m
21-100m   1000m
101-200m   500m
201m+   250m
            Sea Level

9°30'S

116°00'E 116°30'E 117°00'E

Practicalities

Climate

Bali's pleasant tropical climate has become legendary in travelers' circles. Though it is warm year-round, humidity and rainfall vary dramatically. The cooler, breezy dry season, from April to October, is the best time to visit. Humidity is low and temperatures range from 20°C (68°F) at night to 30°C (85°F) during the day. The rest of the year is more humid and cloudier and has more rainstorms, but is still bearable. November and December are typically the rainiest months. It can be cool in the evenings from June through October, especially along the beaches and at higher elevations.

You can dive year-round in Bali, though the visibility near river mouths decreases during the rainy months. Water temperatures range from 21 to 31°C (70 to 88°F), with the warmest waters occurring during the summer months, December to March. Between August and December, upwellings can cause the temperatures to drop. This is especially common at Nusa Penida, Lembongan, Candidasa and Padangbai.

Lombok's dry season is from June to October. The wet season (October to May) is a little hotter and considerably more humid, but in some ways it's more pleasant, as the landscape is greener and more attractive. Most divers head to the Gili Islands, off Lombok's northwest shore, where it is warm year-round. A light trade wind blows from late June to November.

Diving is year-round in the Gilis. Even during the rainy season, you'll find excellent diving, as this is often when you'll see manta rays. Runoff after a big rain may reduce visibility. Water temperatures range from 26 to 31°C (79 to 88°F), depending on the time of year.

Language

Bahasa Indonesia is the national language. Most people in Bali speak both Bahasa Indonesia and the indigenous language, Bahasa Bali. English is common in tourist areas. Lombok residents speak Bahasa Indonesia and Bahasa Sasak. English is also spoken in a few of Lombok's tourist areas, particularly in the Gili Islands.

Visitors will get along using just a few Bahasa Indonesia phrases. Even if the words come out wrong, local residents appreciate it when visitors try to speak their language.

Useful Bahasa Indonesia Phrases

English	Bahasa	Pronunciation
Hello	Selamat	Sell-ah-mot
Good morning	Selamat pagi	Sell-ah-mot Pah-gee
Where are you from?	Dari mana Anda?	Dah-ree Mah-nah
Where are you going?	Mau ke mana?	Mah-ow kay Mah-nah
What is your name?	Siapa nama Anda?	See-ah-puh Nah-mah Ahn-dah

Useful Phrases for Divers

English	Bahasa
Which way does the current go?	Ke mana arus pergi?
The current is going...	Arus ke...
...right	...kanan
...left	...kiri
...up	...naik
...down	...turun
Is there a strong current?	Arus keras sekali?
The current is (not) strong	Arus (tidak) keras
How is the visibility?	Bagaimana cuaca (*or* kelihatan) didalam?
Are there dangerous animals?	Ada binatang bahia didalam?
How deep will we dive?	Berapa dalam mau kita diving?
How long will we dive?	Berapa lama menyalam?
We will dive to ___ meters	Kita mau diving ___
The air is no good	Angin tidak bagus
Where is the boat?	Di mana jukung/kapal (*or* boat)?
The boat will pick us up...	Kapal jemput saya...
Stop the motor, please	Stop motor (*or* stop mesin), terima kasih
Do you have a...?	Ada...?
Is there oxygen on the boat?	Ada oxigan di boat?

safety sausage	pelampung
current	arus
strong current	arus keras (kuat)
careful	hati-hati
water	air
high tide	air pasang
low tide	air surut
dive	selam

Women and children can be seen walking to temple, their elaborate offerings balanced on their heads.

Getting There

Diving & Flying

Most divers in Indonesia arrive by plane. While it's fine to dive soon *after* flying, it's important to remember that your last dive should be completed at least 12 hours (some experts advise 24 hours, particularly after repetitive dives) *before* your flight to minimize the risk of decompression sickness, caused by residual nitrogen in the blood.

Most international visitors fly in to either Bali or Jakarta. There are direct flights to both from numerous European and Asian capitals, with the cheapest fares generally from London and Bangkok. Flights from the U.S. are generally via Guam, Japan, Korea, Taiwan or Hong Kong. There are also direct flights from all of Australia's international airports.

Bali's airport is in Ngurah Rai, just 2.5km (1.5 miles) south of the Kuta-Legian district, but the airport is often referred to internationally as Denpasar, or DPS. There are direct domestic flights between Ngurah Rai, Bali, and Mataram, Lombok. Be sure to confirm bookings at least 72 hours before departure.

There are two ferries a day between the eastern Balinese port of Padangbai and Lembar on the west coast of Lombok. The crossing takes at least four hours.

Slow-paced farming communities are just a short drive from the bustle of Kuta-Legian.

A powered catamaran (the air-conditioned *Bounty*) also operates twice daily between Benoa in southern Bali and Lombok's Senggigi. The *Bounty* takes less than three hours to cross.

Gateway City – Kuta-Legian

Kuta-Legian is Bali's main tourism center and is where most visiting divers stay, eat and party, at least upon arrival or departure. To get here from the Ngurah Rai airport, simply pay the set price to your destination at the official taxi counter, or (a less simple option if you have lots of dive gear) walk across the parking lot and hail a metered cab.

Kuta isn't pretty, but it's not dull either. In many ways, it is still a village—a place of quiet compounds and narrow *gangs* (alleys) where devotional offerings are placed in front of houses and neighbors emerge into the coolness of the evening to gossip in the street.

Behind the beaches, a labyrinth of roads and alleys leads to an amazing clutch of hotels, restaurants, bars, food stalls and shops. Kuta provides a range of accommodations and cuisine, great shopping, surf, sunsets and riotous nightlife. It is unabashedly, crassly commercial, but the cosmopolitan mixture of beach-party hedonism, loose anarchy and entrepreneurial energy can be exciting.

Most places in Kuta-Legian can be reached on foot, but taxis are ubiquitous and useful for when you get tired of trudging. Crime is not a major problem, but pickpocketing (especially from backpacks) is increasingly common. Be especially careful late at night.

If you're heading out for a dive trip, Kuta-Legian is a good place to change money, buy groceries, sundries and toiletries, and stock up on batteries and film.

Getting Around

Taxis are plentiful in the southern tourist destinations and can be called to most locations, but it helps to have good directions if you are not staying in a well-known hotel. This may require the help of someone conversant in Bahasa Indonesia. Local cab drivers are usually dependable and can even be quite colorful. Make sure you tell your driver to start the meter when you get in, or you may wind up in difficult and costly negotiations at the end of your ride. If you like your driver, you can arrange to be dropped off and picked up later if you want to go clubbing. Be sure to work out how much you'll pay for this convenience prior to making the deal.

The main forms of public transport on Bali are the cheap buses and minibuses (called *bemos*) that run on more or less set routes within or between towns. They are difficult to use if you're carrying dive gear. Tourist shuttle buses, which run between the major tourist centers, are more expensive than public transport but are also more comfortable and convenient.

You can rent cars, motorbikes and bemos (with or without drivers) through hotels, travel agents and street-side entrepreneurs. Remember that the Balinese drive on the left, use their horns a lot and give way to traffic pulling onto the road.

Lombok has an extensive network of roads, but public buses and bemos are generally restricted to main routes. If you prefer to explore on your own, you can rent a car or motorbike, or charter a bemo.

Frequent shuttle boats service the Gili Islands. No cars or motorbikes are allowed on the Gilis, so walking, bicycle and *cidomo* (horse and cart) are the only modes of transport.

Around both Bali and Lombok, outrigger boats called *jukungs* are used for short trips to snorkeling spots or surf breaks, while slightly larger boats travel between islands.

Ferries make island hopping easy, while traditional jukung boats might take you to a local diving or snorkeling spot.

Entry

Upon entry, you must present a passport that is valid for at least six months from the date of your arrival, and an onward or return ticket (which may be purchased at the point of entry). Tourist visas are issued when you arrive and are valid for 60 days. Visitors from countries not eligible for tourist visas may have to pay an entry fee. Contact your Indonesian embassy or consulate to find out if you are eligible for a tourist visa.

Still and video cameras, radio cassette recorders, computers, and most other electronic and sports equipment must be declared on arrival and leave with you on departure.

A departure tax must be paid in cash when you check-in to depart. Credit cards are not accepted, so have enough cash on hand. To get into the departure lounge, you must have a departure-tax receipt attached to your boarding pass.

Time

Bali is eight hours ahead of GMT. No adjustment is made for daylight saving time. Accordingly, during standard time, noon in Bali is 2pm in Sydney, 4am in London and 8pm the previous day in San Francisco.

Money

The rupiah is Indonesia's official currency. Its value changes almost daily, sometimes greatly. Money exchange offices are the best bet for getting a favorable exchange rate, as banks tend to offer rates that are more conservative. Bring your own calculator because some money changers have altered units. Count your money in front of the cashier and don't leave before getting the proper count.

There are no banks on Lombok's Gili Islands, but there are exchange offices. They don't offer as favorable an exchange rate as you can find on a main island such as Bali or Lombok, so it is best to bring rupiah with you. Blue Marlin Dive Center will exchange money for its clients at favorable rates.

Traveler's checks and credit cards are accepted at most hotels, restaurants and dive shops, but it is wise to ask before purchasing anything. Generally, traveler's checks are exchanged at a lower rate than cash. Visa and MasterCard are the most widely accepted credit cards, and American Express is accepted to a lesser extent. Be prepared to pay a 3% to 6% credit card service fee.

Electricity

European standard 220V AC electricity is the norm in Bali and Lombok. Some small villages may still use 110V, but this is not common. Plugs and outlets are set up for two round pins. Wall outlets are deeply recessed, however, so an adapter may be needed for some chargers and converters. Be sure to bring both an adapter and a converter if you will need to charge lights or batteries.

Weights & Measures

The metric system is standard throughout Indonesia. All retail and rental dive gear use metric measurements. In this book, both metric and imperial measurements are given, except for specific references within dive site descriptions, which are given in metric units only. See the conversion chart on the inside back cover for imperial equivalents.

What to Bring

Clothes shopping is a real bargain in Bali, so some people bring an empty suitcase and buy all of their tropical wear here. Lightweight, informal clothing is best suited to Bali and Lombok's warm and tropical climate. Hats, sunglasses and sunscreen are recommended and are generally available throughout the islands. Sunscreen with a high sun protection factor may not be available, so consider bringing your own. A long-sleeved T-shirt or light jacket will help keep you warm when cool evening sea breezes blow.

Island style prevails: Cool, loose-fitting clothing is acceptable in most places. Formal wear is unnecessary and impractical. Though swimsuits are fine on the boats and beaches, swimsuits and short shorts are inappropriate in towns, villages, temples or public buildings. Women should wear a sarong or skirt to cover their thighs. Topless sunbathing is acceptable only at hotel pools and a few public beaches (Kuta-Legian, Sanur and Nusa Dua). Other places, keep your suit on.

Bali and Lombok's waters are warm, so a dive skin or 1 to 3mm wetsuit is adequate thermal protection for most divers. Both retail and rental diving gear are available in Bali and (on a limited basis) on Lombok's Gili Islands, but, when possible, it is best to bring your own gear. Weights, belts and tanks are always provided on dive trips. For those traveling with metric gear, DIN adapters are available on a limited basis. It is best to carry your own. Also, don't forget to pack a safety sausage.

Repair services are available for many brands of gear. **Divemasters Bali** (Jalan Bypass I Gusti Ngurah Rai #61XX, Sanur, ☎ (361) 289028) is one of the best-stocked dive stores and offers some equipment repair. Also, **Dive Indonesia (Bali Surf 'n Dive Center)** has opened a store (7 Pantai Kuta, Kuta, ☎ (361) 766888 or 764888) and plans to open more.

Underwater Photography

You won't find much professional underwater photo equipment for sale in Bali or Lombok, but you will find point-and-shoot cameras designed for snorkeling or shallow diving. Film and batteries, including high-quality alkalines, are readily available. That said, if you are a serious photographer, it is best to bring everything you need. Digital prints and system processing are not available in Bali or Lombok at this time.

Bali Fotografi (57X Jalan Raya, Kuta, ☎ (361) 751329) offers reliable E6 processing. See the personable and capable manager, Leo Tlimewu, if you need special film, a rush job, push processing or any other special service.

Business Hours

In Kuta and most tourist-oriented areas, business hours are typically 10am to 9pm, Monday through Saturday. Most retail stores are open limited hours on

Sundays. Stores at more remote destinations (such as many of the dive areas) stay open until about 8pm. Banks and government offices are closed on weekends. Restaurants and bars are open until midnight and sometimes later. In Kuta, many bars and eateries are open all night, especially on the weekends.

Accommodations

Bali has accommodations to suit every budget and desire. Bali's opulent top-end hotels host the rich and famous from all reaches of the globe. But even dirt-cheap accommodations are generally clean and comfortable. If you plan on staying at upper-echelon hotels during peak seasons (July through early September and mid-December through January), be sure to make a reservation.

Many dive shops have package deals with the nicer hotels and offer convenient shuttle service. A few boutique hotels cater especially to divers: Gear is stored on the premises and marine-life reference books are available so divers can find out what they just saw on the reef.

You'll find rather posh, private dive retreats among Bali's accommodations options.

Dining & Food

Bali's restaurants offer an eclectic mix of cuisine in a range of prices—from the street-side food stands that charge a pittance for an array of tasty food to the five-star hotels that offer some of the planet's best meals at equally astronomical prices. Fresh local seafood is the highlight of many menus. Out of the main tourist areas, the selection of restaurants is somewhat limited, but ask around, as there are often some nice surprises where you least expect them.

Fresh seafood is offered at many of Bali's coastal eateries.

Tipping your server is optional but appreciated, especially at the smaller restaurants. At larger or more expensive restaurants, a service charge or gratuity is often included in the bill, so check before you tip.

A cheap and convenient option is to buy bottled water, soft drinks and alcoholic drinks, as well as basic foodstuffs and snacks, from a local store. You may even be able to do this between dives, as most boat drivers return to shore if the dive site is nearby.

Shopping

Watch your bank account—Bali is *the* shopper's paradise! From cheap clothing to furniture to video games, you can buy almost anything here. Kuta has the biggest variety and best prices for general souvenirs, but if you have specific purchases in mind, you might want to plan your shopping frenzy ahead of time.

Celuk is still the best place to buy jewelry and silver. There are many manufacturers and a lot of competition, so with a bit of bargaining you can get some great deals. The same applies for wood carvings in the nearby village of Mas. Both villages are very close to Ubud, which is also a shopper's heaven. Ubud's many shops and stands are now complemented by a few upscale clothing and contemporary Balinese art boutiques, which have opened in recent years. You'll likely find the atmosphere more relaxing than Kuta's, although there isn't as wide a selection of goods for sale.

If you don't want to spend too much time hunting for souvenirs, your best bet is to stroll along Kuta-Legian's Jalan Legian. This 4km (2½ mile) long street stretches from the famous Bemo Corner all the way to Seminyak. The farther north you head the more upmarket the merchandise is.

Don't be shy about bargaining—it is an art that becomes fun after a little bit of practice. The key is to not make your initial offer so low that you insult the seller. Generally, start by offering a little more than half the price asked. Many shops (generally fancy-looking air-conditioned places that accept credit cards) have fixed prices.

Boycotting Marine Products

Many marine products are taken from Indonesia's waters to sell locally and internationally. Collecting shells, corals, sea fans, turtle shells and fish has a profound impact on the ecological balance and health of the reef system, and detracts from the natural beauty of the reef. Most collection methods—such as the use of cyanide or curtain nets—destroy the marine habitat and deplete slow-growing species and their reproductive populations.

You can discourage collection from Indonesia's reefs by not purchasing marine products, opting instead for locally produced crafts that represent the county's rich cultural diversity. Your purchasing choices both in Indonesia and at home, combined with government regulation and enforcement, can help restore and maintain reef populations.

Activities & Attractions

The variety of activities in Bali is part of what makes it such an attractive vacation spot. From exciting and physically challenging outdoor adventures to a relaxing day of shopping followed by a massage on the beach, Bali has something for everyone.

The island's incredible climate and scenery make it an ideal place to explore while hiking, biking, skydiving, or riding a horse or elephant, or by a number of other usual and unusual methods. Regardless of the activity, be sure to ask about what kind of insurance the company has for its customers. Also, ensure that your guide is experienced and knowledgeable—a trained guide is often the key to an entertaining and educational outing.

Most importantly, leave Bali the way you would like others to find it: beautiful and unspoiled.

Hiking

Hiking is a popular way to see Bali's jungles and rice paddies. Visitors have all kinds of options, from short half-day walks to strenuous multiday treks. The northwestern part of Bali is at its greenest and park hikes are at their best at the end of the rainy season, in March or April. The Gunung Batukau area has a variety of flora and fauna, such as ancient strangler trees, ferns, wild orchids and hanging liana, as well as tropical birds, monkeys, wild boar and deer. For an unbeatable hike high in the central ranges of west Bali, join an 8km (5-mile) jungle trek led by experienced and multilingual guides through virgin tropical rainforest. A number of adventure companies offer village and mountain treks and can organize specialized group tours.

Paddy Treks

A rice paddy trek is a popular way to get a glimpse of traditional rural Balinese life. One spectacular area is the Carang Sari rice bowl, an hour's drive northeast of Kuta. The three-hour walk through the beautiful Ayung River valley is suitable for the whole family. Trekkers follow farmers' tracks through emerald green paddies, where they observe the timeless work of plowing, planting and harvesting using handcrafted tools and age-old techniques. Along the path, you will see coconut, mango and jackfruit plantations, as well as village temples. Treks finish at the village of Kedewatan just northwest of Ubud.

Elephant Trekking

You can see Bali from the back of an elephant at the **Elephant Safari Park**, in the cool jungle of Desa Taro just 20 minutes north of Ubud. The park offers a chance to take a ride and feed, touch and interact with Indonesian elephants, which you'll see cooling off in the park's lake and grazing peacefully. The park's reception center offers information about the history and diversity of the pachyderms.

Indonesian elephants are natives of Sumatra, where their habitat is rapidly dwindling. Consequently, their population is at risk and the animal is now on the endangered species list. There are currently fewer than 1,100 Indonesian elephants left in a wild. The Elephant Safari Park contributes a portion of its proceeds to assist Indonesian elephant breeding and relocation programs.

Elephant treks take riders through jungles and across rice paddies in the scenic Desa Taro.

Climbing

Bali's rugged, high-profile terrain provides numerous places for climbers to explore. Climbs range from novice to expert, but a certain degree of physical fitness is a must, as the rough landscape and altitude can be physically taxing. Bali's highest mountain, Gunung Agung, can take from four to eight hours to climb. Most people start the trek up to the volcanic crater at 3am, when it is coolest, and arrive in time to see the sunrise. Gunung Batur is lower in altitude and a somewhat easier trek that families try. It takes a full day to reach the summit of Gunung Batukau and return. Guides are recommended on all climbing trips. The most challenging climbs are not recommended during the rainy season (November to March).

For experienced rock climbers and those who would just like to give it a shot, Kuta's **Adrenaline Park** offers a state-of-the-art 110 sq m (1,000 sq ft) climbing wall. The facility supplies safety belts and a spotter.

Rafting

River rafting is a fun and exciting way to see Bali's interior. The rainforests and water-carved gorges of the Ayung River (near Ubud) are a popular destination because they are close to the tourist areas, but river trips are offered throughout the island.

Before you set out, outfitters will fit you with a life jacket, helmet and paddle, and typically provide rudimentary instructions on steering. The most frequently toured 11km (7-mile) stretch of river has nearly thirty sets of rapids. The trip is usually suitable for beginners, but conditions can change dramatically after a heavy rainfall. Depending on the conditions, guides will take passengers through rapids, under waterfalls, past temples and along the banks of rice fields and washing areas. Passengers may even have the chance to steer the raft, or "body raft" by hopping in and riding the river. At the end of the expedition, rafters are usually taken to a rest area where they can enjoy a hot shower and a Balinese meal.

Ocean Rafting

Though ocean rafting isn't really an athletic challenge, it's super fast, exhilarating and sometimes wet! If the seas are rough, this can be an amazing adrenaline rush. Big motorboats with inflatable sides and solid bottoms are used to head into the surf, cross the channel and cruise along the cliffs of both Bali and Nusa Penida. **Bali Hai Cruises** at Benoa Harbor operates two fast speedboats—one has three 150hp engines and the other has four whopping 250hp engines.

Bali Hai Cruises offers a morning ocean-rafting trip along the base of the Uluwatu cliffs. This is a great place to see dolphins and whales from August through December. Another daily run (made later in the morning) takes you to the islands of Nusa Lembongan, Nusa Ceningan and Nusa Penida, where you can

An ocean-rafting excursion can take you along the dramatic coastline of Nusa Penida.

explore 100m high coastal cliffs, tour a village or go snorkeling. Passengers sometimes see manta rays and fruit-bat colonies at Bat Rock (southern Nusa Penida).

Mountain Biking

Guided mountain-bike rides can be fun for the whole family. Tour operators usually provide transport to the trailhead, mountain bikes, guides and water for the trip.

The Batur Trail starts in Kintamani and descends along secluded paths through central Bali. You'll ride through rainforest, stands of bamboo, incredible rice terraces and quiet highland villages. A stop at one of the family farms allows riders to meet villagers and see some of the crops. The trail ends in Ubud, where an Indonesian lunch is served at a restaurant overlooking a river gorge. This downhill ride is a great way to take in the sights, sounds and smells of Bali without getting caught in traffic. Your hands may get tired from braking, but it is easy on the legs.

Cycling through rural Bali allows you to see farms and villages.

There is also a longer ride starting high in the mountains at the village of Mayungan. This 25km (16 mile) ride winds its way down along valleys, passing temples and shrines and crisscrossing rice fields.

Surfing

Bali is known as a surfer's paradise and all levels of wave-riders show up here. The consistent ocean swells give the island great surf breaks nearly year-round.

The long rolling waves, sandy seafloor and qualified instructors make Bali's Kuta Beach a good place to learn to surf. Two-hour group lessons start in a swimming pool where you'll learn water safety, surf etiquette, board handling and surfing basics. The lesson continues at the beach, where a team of coaches works to help potential surfers get up on a board and ride a wave. Tuition normally includes safe-learner surfboard rental, UV sun protection, a surf shirt and insurance.

Experienced surfers can try their luck with the bigger waves and trickier surf breaks at Uluwatu.

Skydiving

Those who try skydiving normally come away from the experience quite exhilarated. A tandem jump with an experienced instructor begins with a safety briefing and 30-minute introduction to the sport. The jumper is then fitted with a harness and taken to the aircraft. The aircraft climbs to approximately 3,000m (10,000ft), where the instructor attaches his harness. Together you jump from the aircraft and immediately experience free-fall parachuting. After free falling for nearly 2,000m (6,000ft), the instructor pulls the rip cord and the main parachute fills with air. The amazing 180km/h (112mph) free fall slows to a relaxing 20km/h (12mph) drop. The instructor takes control of the parachute to ensure a safe and comfortable landing.

Tandem jumps usually include air-conditioned round-trip transportation to the departure site, all equipment and US$100,000 insurance coverage. You will not be permitted to skydive if you have been scuba diving within the last 24 hours. Other restrictions may also apply.

JIMMY HALL/SEA TO SKY

Chuted sports like paragliding (shown here) and
tandem skydiving are becoming popular Bali endeavors.

Diving Health & Safety

General Health

Bali is a generally healthy place to travel, but it is worth taking a few precautions before and during your trip. A yellow-fever vaccination certificate is required for travelers coming from infected areas. Malaria is not present in the main tourist areas of Java and Bali, the Jakarta municipality or Lombok's Gili Islands. If you plan to travel outside of these malaria-free areas, consult your physician about anti-malaria medication and other preventive tactics well before your departure. Amoebic and bacillary dysenteries are present. Hepatitis A and E occur and hepatitis B is hyperendemic.

The most important health rule is to be careful about what you eat and drink—stomach upsets are the most common health problem for travelers. Food is one of the many joys of traveling here, but it is also a potential source of problems, so a bit of caution is in order. Thoroughly cooked food is safest, and fruit that can be peeled is also a safe bet.

Drink only bottled, purified water and avoid ice that is not made from purified water. Also be sure you drink enough—dehydration can be a big problem in the tropics and is often a contributing factor to decompression sickness.

The U.S. Centers for Disease Control & Prevention regularly posts updates on health-related concerns around the world specifically for travelers. Call (toll-free from the U.S.) ☎ 888-232-3299 and request Document 000005 to receive a list of documents available by fax. The website is www.cdc.gov.

Pre-Trip Preparation

Your general state of health, diving skill level and specific equipment needs are the three most important factors that impact any dive trip. If you honestly assess these before you leave, you'll be well on your way to assuring a safe dive trip.

First, if you're not in shape, start exercising. Second, if you haven't dived for a while (six months is too long) and your skills are rusty, do a local dive with an experienced buddy or take a scuba review course. Finally, inspect your dive gear. Feeling good physically and diving with experience and reliable equipment will not only increase your safety, but also enhance your enjoyment underwater.

At least a month before your trip, inspect your dive gear. Remember, your regulator should be serviced annually, whether you've used it or not. If you use a dive computer and can replace the battery yourself, change it before the trip or buy a spare one to take along. Otherwise, send the computer to the manufacturer for a battery replacement.

If possible, find out if the dive center rents or services the type of gear that you own. If not, you might want to take spare parts or even spare gear. A spare mask is always a good idea. A marker tube (also known as a safety sausage or come-to-me) should be considered standard equipment. Buy one if you don't have one.

Do a thorough gear check before heading off on a dive trip.

Purchase any additional equipment you might need, such as a dive light and tank marker light for night diving, a line reel for wreck diving, etc. Make sure you have at least a whistle attached to your BC.

About a week before taking off, do a final check of your gear, grease o-rings, check batteries and assemble a save-a-dive kit. This kit should at minimum contain extra mask and fin straps, snorkel keeper, mouthpiece, valve cap, zip ties and o-rings. Don't forget to pack a first-aid kit and medications such as decongestants, ear drops, antihistamines and seasickness tablets.

Medical & Recompression Facilities

You'll find first-aid supplies and over-the-counter and prescription medications at local pharmacies throughout Bali and Lombok. Look for the *apotek* (sometimes spelled *apotik*) sign on the building. Be aware that the contents and directions for taking most medications are written in Bahasa Indonesia, so make sure you know what you're getting as well as how to administer it.

You can seek treatment for minor ailments at local clinics in the tourist areas, but the level of care and diagnosis can be questionable. More reputable is the **Bali International Medical Center** (BIMC; Jalan Bypass Ngurah Rai #1000X, Kuta 80361, ☎ (361) 761263, fax (361) 764345, bimc@dps.meganet.id). It is open 24 hours and offers consultations; preventive, urgent and emergency care; and full medical reporting for insurance companies.

Also getting high marks is the **International SOS 24 Hour Medical Clinic** (Jalan Bypass Ngurah Rai #24X, Kuta 80361, 24-hour emergency ☎ (361) 755768, Administration ☎ (361) 764515, Clinic ☎ (361) 764555, fax (361) 764530, jwintsos@indosat.net.id). Hospitals in Denpasar and Singaraja are also equipped to handle most medical problems. Fees must be paid before leaving the hospital.

In the case of a diving emergency, call the **Sanglah Hospital** in Denpasar at ☎ (361) 227911 through -915. Ask for the **Hyperbaric Chamber Unit** (*Ruang Hiperbarik* in Bahasa Indonesia). They will arrange to stabilize and evacuate the victim. If no one answers at the Hyperbaric Chamber Unit, call the unit head, Dr. Antonius Natasamudra, at home (☎ (361) 420842). In the rare event that the Denpasar chamber is not operating, the victim will be transferred to the chamber in Surabaya, Java. Health insurance that includes emergency repatriation coverage is strongly advised.

DAN

Divers Alert Network (DAN) is an international membership association of individuals and organizations sharing a common interest in diving and safety. It includes DAN Southeast Asia and Pacific (DAN SEAP), an autonomous nonprofit organization based in Australia. DAN operates a 24-hour diving emergency hotline. DAN SEAP members should call ☎ **61 8 8212 9242**. DAN America members should call ☎ **919-684-8111** or **919-684-4DAN** (-4326). The latter accepts collect calls in a dive emergency. Though DAN does not directly provide medical care, it does provide advice on early treatment, evacuation and hyperbaric treatment of diving-related injuries. Divers should contact DAN for assistance as soon as a diving emergency is suspected.

DAN membership is reasonably priced and includes DAN TravelAssist, a membership benefit that covers medical air evacuation from anywhere in the world for any illness or injury. For a small additional fee, divers can get secondary insurance coverage for decompression illness. For membership questions, contact DAN at ☎ 800-446-2671 in the U.S. or ☎ 919-684-2948 elsewhere. DAN can also be reached at www.diversalertnetwork.org.

Signaling Devices

SARAH J. H. HUBBARD

One of the greatest dangers of open-water diving is the possibility of drifting away at the surface without being seen. Make sure this never happens to you! A diver is extremely difficult to locate in the water, so always dive with a signaling device of some sort, preferably more than one.

One good signaling device that is also the easiest to carry is a whistle—even the little ones are quite effective. Use a zip tie to attach one permanently to your BC. Even better, though more expensive, is a loud horn that connects to the inflator hose. To operate it, simply push a button to let out a blast. It does require air from your tank to function, though.

It is imperative that you can be seen as well as heard. One of the most important pieces of dive equipment to carry is a marker tube, pictured here. The best ones are bright in color and about 3m (10ft) long. They roll up and will easily fit into a BC pocket or clip onto a D-ring. They are inflated orally or with a regulator. Some allow you to insert a dive light into the tube—a nice feature when it is dark.

Other signaling aides include mirrors, flares and dye markers, but these have limited reliability. A simple dive light is particularly versatile. Not only can it be used during the day for looking into crevices and crannies, but it also comes in handy for nighttime signaling.

Diving in Bali & Lombok

Bali and Lombok's spectacular marine environment boasts more than 2,500 fish species and an uncountable number of corals and invertebrates. Scientists continue to discover new species here, some of which are believed to be endemic. The islands' rich biodiversity is one of their many blessings—this small area may well represent the most biologically diverse undersea environment on Earth.

Bali is a haven for serious underwater photographers and critter lovers, who will find macro subjects like shrimp, mandarinfish and rare nudibranchs. While many of Bali's most abundant species are small, divers may also be rewarded with big-animal action. On the larger end of the scale, migrating whales, mantas, mobulas, dolphins, whale sharks, hammerhead sharks, tiger sharks and even orcas cruise through Bali's waters on occasion. You may even catch a glimpse of an unusual mola-mola (a large, oceanic sunfish with an unusual disk-shaped body), which typically come to the area during the winter.

Map Index

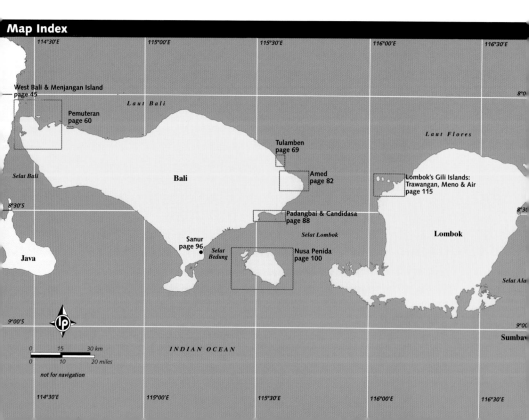

Rebounding Reefs

Coral bleaching occurs when corals are under severe stress, which can be induced by a variety of factors. Extreme temperatures and increased UV rays are the two most common causes, but disease, chemicals, salinity and exposure to air and rain at extreme low tides can also be significant. Global oceanic warming occurred during El Niño weather patterns in 1997 and '98, causing bleaching along many coral reefs in the Indo-Pacific, including some of Bali's reefs.

Warm waters have bleached some corals.

A change in water temperature causes corals to shed some or all of their zooxanthellae, the single-celled plant that lives in the coral's tissue. Zooxanthellae not only provide the coral with nutrients through photosynthesis, but also give the coral its color. When they are shed, the colony appears to go white. Corals can recover if the stress is not extreme and if the few remaining zooxanthellae reproduce and reestablish the symbiotic relationship.

Divers will see evidence of coral bleaching in some places in Bali. Upper reef areas at Menjangan, Pemuteran, Tulamben and Amed were hit to varying degrees. Other sites were affected minimally or not at all. The reefs fed by currents and upwellings (at Nusa Penida, Lembongan, Candidasa and Padangbai) show virtually no problems resulting from El Niño.

The most noticeable damage is seen on the reeftop table and platter corals. In some places, more aggressive and heartier corals have taken over the coral skeletons. Encrusting sponges and some algae have also moved in to take advantage of this newly available reef area.

The new polyps and formations make interesting macrophotography subjects. The sea anemones, which also turn white during elevated water temperatures, can be quite beautiful. The coral skeletons have also become refuges for fish and invertebrates.

A unique coral regrowth program that uses electrolysis was started in 2000 in Pemuteran and is already showing promising results.

Diving and snorkeling in Bali and Lombók provides a chance to see both the marine life and the varied underwater topography that this area offers. Dive sites range from calm and colorful near-shore swims to thrilling current-swept walls. Most dives are shallow enough for divers of every skill level to enjoy, and include extremely colorful fish life and a variety of hard and soft corals. Mild currents can be expected at many sites.

Though surfers and tourists love Bali's southwest coast, the high surf usually makes the area too rough for diving. Most dive sites are on Bali's less exposed east and northwest coasts, around Nusa Penida, Nusa Lembongan and tiny Nusa Ceningan, and in Lombok's Gili Islands. Shore dives are quite common in a few regions, and most boat dives are less than 15 minutes' travel time by local outrigger.

Many of the better dive regions have nearby accommodations and facilities suitable for divers, ranging from basic bungalows to upscale resorts that feature rooms with a private pool or lotus pond. Staying locally is a good option for a peaceful vacation that includes diving and other outdoor activities along with cultural excursions to barong dance performances and local temples.

For those who want to add shopping and nightlife to their vacation itineraries, southern Bali's stretch of coast between Kuta and Legian is a popular tourist area, and Seminyak, Sanur and Nusa Dua are also good options. Divers based here rise early to travel two to four hours by bemo to dive sites in Padangbai, Candidasa, Tulamben and Menjangan. If this is your first time in Bali, this is a fun way to see the villages and countryside. However, the increasing traffic between Kuta and Klungkung (to the northeast) makes the trip slower and less pleasant, with produce trucks belching black diesel fumes as they move along at a snail's pace. Make sure your bemo is air-conditioned. Divers generally return before sunset to enjoy the nightlife of these tourist centers.

A popular alternative to the traffic and smog are the two- to five-day diving "safaris." These safaris enable divers to take overnight trips to various dive regions or combine two or three popular areas. Divers stay in a nice hotel and make repetitive dives on the best reefs without a long daily commute. These trips are organized through many local dive shops. For best results, email ahead with a rough itinerary to see if your plans are realistic and to ensure a booking.

Divers prepare to practice new skills in the safety of a resort pool.

Diving in Lombok is done around the three scenic Gili Islands just north of Senggigi. The Gili Islands are Lombok's best dive destination for several reasons. Lombok's current economy and political strife have slowed the development of its mainland dive businesses for the time being. Also, dynamite and cyanide fishing have been problems along Lombok's coast and are still not under control.

Most divers feel that the Gili's white-sand beaches,

palm trees and unpaved streets add up to paradise. The only lookout on these flat little isles is a hill on Trawangan, where locals grow tapioca and graze goats. Underwater, Lombok's Gili Islands are edged with sloping reefs. Divers can explore canyons and walls north of Gili Air and along the Lombok coast. The bay between the Gili Islands and Lombok holds the remains of several ships that met their demise along the shallow shore. Slowly but surely, local dive operators are finding these wrecks, as well as good deep-water reef sites, and continue to look for shallow sites that have not been damaged by dynamite fishing.

You can reach the Gili Islands in as little as two and a half hours by the Bounty's fast boat, or you can opt for a slower boat that leaves from the docks in Benoa and Padangbai. Because of the relatively long travel times from Bali, most divers plan to stay in the Gili Islands or check into the upscale resorts at mainland Senggigi.

Though diving in Bali and Lombok is underrated by some—it has to compete with so many other tourist activities—it lives up to the standards of a world-class dive destination in many respects. The variety of accommodations and activities, the range of reef topography and dive conditions, the presence of a few wrecks, and, of course, the diversity of species seen by day and by night contribute to its growing status as one of the world's most popular dive destinations.

Snorkeling

Snorkeling is a popular activity around Bali, Nusa Penida and Lombok's Gili Islands. Colorful shallow corals and abundant marine life are often just a short swim or boat ride from shore. Most snorkeling is done independently, although it is possible to join a dive boat and snorkel above the divers. Rates for these trips are usually cheaper for snorkelers than divers. Be sure to keep an eye out for currents if you are venturing from shore. Some areas have strong inshore currents. Snorkeling gear is available from most hotels, but bring your own if you want to be sure you're happy with your gear.

Top 10 Snorkeling Sites

5	Temple Slopes, East Menjangan Island
13	Kebun Chris, Pemuteran
17	*Liberty* Wreck, Tulamben
18	Tulamben House Reef, Tulamben
20	Tulamben Dropoff, Tulamben
27	Amed Coral Gardens, Amed
38	Lembongan Marine Park, Nusa Lembongan
46	S.D. (Sekolah Desar), Nusa Penida
47	Pura Ped, Nusa Penida
58	Frogfish Reef (Manuk Brie), Gili Air

Dive Training & Certification

Divers and snorkelers of all experience levels can enjoy Bali and Lombok's underwater offerings. You'll find novice, intermediate, advanced, specialty, nitrox and technical diving options. A few years ago, rental equipment was not of the highest standard, but that is rapidly changing and most dive shops now carry reliable and modern gear.

People often learn to dive here, and many instructors bring groups to Bali for advanced training. Courses are offered at most tourist areas, and dive hotels usually have an instructor on hand. Courses can be completed in three to five days. Currently, PADI is the only certifying agency in Bali. Its representative makes regular visits to confirm that the shops meet PADI standards. Many resorts display a PADI sign, but you should check that the facility has a current affiliation certificate.

Dive Site Icons

The symbols at the beginning of each dive site description provide a quick summary of some of the important characteristics of each site:

 Good snorkeling or free-diving site.

 Remains or partial remains of a wreck can be seen at this site.

 Sheer wall or drop-off.

 Deep dive. Features of this dive are found in water deeper than 27m (90ft).

 Strong currents may be encountered at this site.

 Strong surge (the horizontal movement of water caused by waves) may be encountered at this site.

 Drift dive. Because of strong currents and/or difficulty in anchoring, a drift dive is recommended at this site.

 Shore dive. This site can be accessed from shore.

 Poor visibility. The site often has visibility of less than 8m (25ft).

 Caves or caverns are prominent features of this site. Only experienced cave divers should explore inner cave areas.

 Marine preserve. Special protective regulations apply in this area.

Pisces Rating System for Dives & Divers

The dive sites in this book are rated according to the following diver skill-level rating system. These are not absolute ratings but apply to divers at a particular time, diving at a particular place. For instance, someone unfamiliar with prevailing conditions might be considered a novice diver at one dive area, but an intermediate diver at another, more familiar location.

Novice: A novice diver should be accompanied by an instructor, divemaster or advanced diver on all dives. A novice diver generally fits the following profile:
◆ basic scuba certification from an internationally recognized certifying agency
◆ dives infrequently (less than one trip a year)
◆ logged fewer than 25 total dives
◆ little or no experience diving in similar waters and conditions
◆ dives no deeper than 18m (60ft)

Intermediate: An intermediate diver generally fits the following profile:
◆ may have participated in some form of continuing diver education
◆ logged between 25 and 100 dives
◆ dives no deeper than 40m (130ft)
◆ has been diving in similar waters and conditions within the last six months

Advanced: An advanced diver generally fits the following profile:
◆ advanced certification
◆ has been diving for more than two years and logged over 100 dives
◆ has been diving in similar waters and conditions within the last six months

Regardless of your skill level, you should be in good physical condition and know your limitations. If you are uncertain of your own level of expertise for a particular site, ask the advice of a local dive instructor. He or she is best qualified to assess your abilities based on the site's prevailing dive conditions. Ultimately, however, you must decide if you are capable of making a particular dive, a decision that should take into account your level of training, recent experience and physical condition, as well as the conditions at the site. Remember that conditions can change at any time, even during a dive.

West Bali & Menjangan Island Dive Sites

West Bali dive sites generally offer clear water, colorful marine life and mild conditions suitable for divers of all levels. Divers who like wall diving will love the region's prime spots around Menjangan Island, but everyone will find something of interest here, with a deep wreck dive, a few unique night dives and many snorkeling sites to choose from.

Most of the region's dive sites are found around Menjangan Island, which is within the boundaries of the Taman Nasional Bali Barat (West Bali National Park). Diving here is regulated. Permits must be obtained through dive shops and diving is done during the day only. Spearfishing is not allowed and all marine life is protected.

Menjangan is an undeveloped wildlife area that is home to the few endangered and endemic Bali starlings left in the wild. The volcanic peaks of Java are clearly visible from the long dock at Labuhan Lalang, where most divers board a boat for the 20-minute trip to the island's south side. The dive shop you choose to go with will arrange for your boat trip and a dive pass.

Menjangan's white-sand beaches make a nice place to stop and offgas while you break for lunch. Underwater, the drop-offs along the south shore and an eastern tip facing the Bali Sea are home to lots of colorful small fish and invertebrates, lacy sea

West Bali & Menjangan Island Dive Sites	Good Snorkeling	Novice	Intermediate	Advanced
1 Pos 1	●	●		
2 Cave Point	●	●		
3 Pos 2	●	●		
4 Bat Caves	●	●		
5 Temple Slopes	●	●		
6 Coral Gardens	●	●		
7 Anker Wreck				●
8 Eel Gardens	●	●		
9 Mimpi Bay	●	●		
10 Secret Bay	●	●		

fans and a variety of sponges. The sandy, gradually sloping terrain of Menjangan's north coast is the final resting place of Bali's oldest divable shipwreck, the Anker Wreck. Even large pelagics are sometimes seen at Menjangan—sightings of whales, whale sharks and manta rays are all reported. Drift diving is common, but currents are usually quite tame and all levels of divers can enjoy the attractions.

Secret Bay is partially within the national-park boundaries and Mimpi Bay is within the park. The marine life at these sites is thus protected, and local guides carefully monitor the sites.

The northwest region has had its share of rough luck. El Niño, dynamite fishing and storms have been hard on the corals, especially those near the surface. Overall, however, the marine life is healthy and quite colorful.

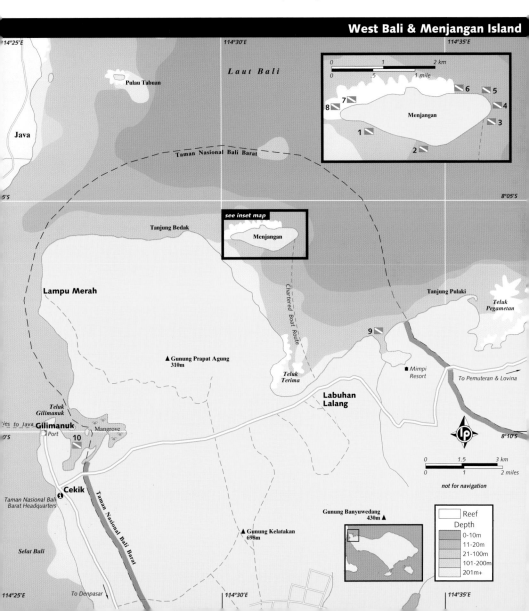

You can reach the northwest from Bali's southern tourist centers in about four hours if you leave early in the morning, five hours if you wait for traffic to mount. If you'd rather spend your time diving than driving, opt for accommodations in nearby Pemuteran or at some of the upscale resorts, such as Mimpi Menjangan Resort, along the Bali coast opposite Menjangan. There are also local hotels in Gilimanuk, and Secret Bay has a small hotel run by Dive & Dives. Pemuteran's dive shops have diving and snorkeling gear for rent and most offer classes. You can arrange (through Dive & Dives) to have rental gear brought to Secret Bay from Sanur. Wetsuits for the bay's cooler waters are available.

1   Pos 1

Pos 1 offers spectacular corals, crevices and fissures, as well as small caves along the reef. You can start this dive from the dive boat, or from shore in front of the now-abandoned park guards' post, where a broad channel leads to the beach. Currents are typically gentle at this site. Batfish often greet divers as

Location: Southwest Menjangan Island

Depth Range: 3-40m (10-130ft)

Access: Shore or boat

Expertise Rating: Novice

Diver examines tube sponge and black-coral trees at Pos 1.

they enter the water. It is hard to miss the abundant fan corals residing along the drop-off and down to 40m or more, but look more closely for sleeping groupers and wary bigeyes in the dark recesses of the reef.

The top of the reef is a good place to see a variety of sea anemones and their clownfish residents, especially spine-cheek anemonefish, which nestle amid the tentacles of their sole host, bubble-tip anemones. You'll also find a plethora of basslets both along the reeftop and amid the black-coral trees. Basslets, also called anthias, are hermaphroditic, born as females but able to assume male characteristics with maturity. It is not unusual to see them in transitional coloration phases. You may catch sight of the brightly colored males displaying their flashy fins.

Sergeant majors and fusiliers are thick along the reeftop. Surgeonfish in powder blues and blacks, emperor angelfish, juvenile and mature wrasse, huge pufferfish, giant sweetlips and lots of other colorful fish also make this stretch of reef their home. Sea fans and fish occupy the current-swept corners of the reef's sandy cuts. Look also for occasional schooling jacks.

The site's biggest disappointment is the damage done by divers who have carved their names or initials into the large sponges. Local guides now discourage this moronic behavior.

Reef Graffiti

Apparently, some divers think it is clever to write their names in Bali's giant sponges. This kind of graffiti damages the marine organisms, takes away from the natural beauty of the reef and spoils the dive for those who care about the environment. Defacing coral and other marine organisms is frowned upon by dive operators and is illegal in the marine parks. Report anyone you see doing this to a park or conservation official. If you notice that a dive guide doesn't take action after seeing a diver damage marine life, report the guide to his or her boss.

2 Cave Point

This site gets its name from the caves along the reef cut at the start of the dive. They are found in 9 to 12m of water and don't penetrate very far into the reef wall, so they are safe to explore. The caves are havens for small fish and invertebrates, like the nudibranchs and schools of tiny baitfish that live amid the black corals and tube sponges.

Location: South Menjangan Island

Depth Range: 3-40m (10-130ft)

Access: Shore or boat

Expertise Rating: Novice

Many crevices house orange-stripe triggerfish, blackspotted pufferfish, soft corals and gorgonian fans. Tubastrea corals occupy many of the cuts and small reef holes from 3 to 9m. Look for crinoids perched atop the sea fans and large sponges that jut out from the wall, as well as tridacna clams and brittle stars. Cave Point also has resident percula clownfish, one-stripe skunk clownfish and spine-cheek anemonefish, along with their associated anemones.

This site is perfect for some challenging and colorful photography. The morning sun can create dramatic lighting situations to enhance photos of reef life and silhouetted divers.

Don't forget to look toward the blue water occasionally, where you may see a seemingly well-fed barracuda cruising the area. Jellyfish sometimes flow in the current here as well.

Colorful macrophotography subjects such as this goby and gorgonian are abundant at Cave Point.

3 Pos 2

This is a very easy beach dive with re-markably distinct terrain on either side of the entry cut. The area to the right (as you face the sea) has steep walls with deep crevices. The area to the left isn't as rugged but provides an endless array of fan corals, some nearly 3m high, in just 9m of water. Lacy gorgonians and delicate black-coral trees adorn the reef. Barrel sponges and immense platter sponges are commonplace. The fish life is active, with schools of yellowtail cascading over the wall. Look for the occasional golden cre-valle jack swimming along the reeftop.

Location: East Menjangan Island

Depth Range: 3-40m (10-130ft)

Access: Shore or boat

Expertise Rating: Novice

Both sides of the cut offer great dis-plays of color, but many divers feel the right side is more impressive. There you'll find many sizes and hues of sea fans with crinoids clinging to their surfaces. This may also be one of the best spots in Indonesia to photograph angelfish, which are abundant and somewhat curious about divers.

Look for lionfish, stonefish and croco-dilefish in the shallows. Small upper-reef corals provide a habitat for juvenile chromis, which hover near the coral heads and seek protection in the branching corals when perceived danger nears.

A diversity of fish flits amid the large stands of sea fans, blue tube sponges and soft corals all along this wall's face. Many clown triggerfish reside here. Titan triggerfish nest at the dive's end (at Men-jangan Island's east tip), so keep alert to avoid get-ting nipped, particularly during mating season (from March to May), when they are most defensive. You may also see a very large moray here.

Pos 2 is a good site for close-up and macrophotography of invertebrates, as there is rarely a current to bother the serious photographer. Also, keep a wide-angle lens handy to capture the blue water's pelagic action, which increases as you near the island's tip. Dolphins have been seen here on occasion and at times accompany the dive boats.

Be careful of the light jellyfish stings, which are carried along with the plank-tonic flow. It is wise to wear a dive skin to prevent getting stung.

Diver and lionfish drift along the wall at Pos 2.

Drift Diving

Drift diving is an integral part of diving in Bali and Lombok, especially around Menjangan Island, Nusa Penida and the Gili Islands. The essential difference between a drift dive and other open-water dives is that on a drift dive, you allow the current to carry you along. Rather than mooring in one place, the dive boat follows your group, picking you up at the end of your dive.

Drift diving can be fun, but divers should be aware of the potential dangers and take extra precautions. Indonesia's dive operators are accustomed to this type of diving and do their best to ensure that you have a safe diving experience. The following tips will help to lessen your likelihood of being the subject of a search-and-rescue mission:

- Drift dives should be undertaken only when the conditions are calm. Rough seas lessen your chances of being seen by the dive boat should you become separated from the group.

- Some sites are subject to up- and down-currents that, though not necessarily dangerous, may prove a bit unsettling. These currents last only a few minutes before reversing or dissipating. Always monitor your depth carefully and adjust your buoyancy accordingly.

- Divers must always carry sufficient signaling devices. You should have a marker tube, a signal light and a whistle. The best marker tubes are brightly colored and about 3m (10ft) high. They roll up and can easily fit into a BC pocket or be clipped onto a D-ring. They're inflated orally or with a regulator.

- Stay with the group. Resist the temptation to dive on your own, as to do so may take you out of sight of the dive boat and cause you to become lost.

- Know your skill level. If you are unsure of your ability to undertake any given dive, consult your divemaster.

- Don't do drift dives at night or during twilight. If you get swept away from your group, the darkness will make it much harder for the dive boat to find you.

4 Bat Caves

The small caves at the waterline of Menjangan Island's easternmost wall are home to a colony of small bats. You'll hear the bats' high-pitched cries as your boat approaches. Snorkelers can go into the caves to have look around, which is a fun and somewhat eerie experience, but the caverns aren't large enough for the average jukung dive boat to enter.

Bat Caves is a continuation of the Pos 2 dive, and is one of the best places to

Location: East Menjangan Island

Depth Range: 3-27m (10-90ft)

Access: Boat

Expertise Rating: Novice

see schools of fish, including fusiliers, pompano, jacks and even albacore tuna, as well as the ever-present schools of tiny silver baitfish. Word has it there is a very old resident great barracuda in the area.

This site is great for snorkeling, as there is a lot of fish action at the reeftop. Look for schooling fish coming into the shallow areas to feed.

Baitfish cluster around black coral at Bat Cave.

5   Temple Slopes

You'll find this sloping dive site just below a small temple overlooking the Bali Sea. Temple Slopes is a great site for all levels of divers. The shallow reeftop (at 5m) is a delight for snorkelers, as thousands of small fish and a variety of sea anemones with their companion clownfish are clearly visible from the surface. Though the 1997 El Niño conditions damaged some of the hard corals, the soft corals have recovered and are healthy and vibrant.

Along the slope, look for soft corals, gorgonians and sponge life. Lobster conceal themselves in the underhangs and under the coral. Look for the blue-

Location: East Menjangan Island

Depth Range: 3-40m (10-130ft)

Access: Boat

Expertise Rating: Novice

spotted rays that like this site's sandy terrain because they can forage for food easily here. Whitetip sharks are sometimes seen resting along the sandy plain at about 30m. The slope eventually dips deeper, but the best scenery is above 20m.

The upper reef makes for a great safety stop. The variety of anemones and clownfish keep most macrophotographers happy. Be sure to check out the commensal shrimp and crabs on the anemones.

6 Coral Gardens

You'll have a clear view of Java and its majestic volcanic craters from this site along the northeastern side of Menjangan Island. This site is a drop-off, though more gradual than the extreme walls of its south-coast counterparts.

The dive starts anywhere along the reeftop in about 6m of water. Check the current before diving in and choose your entry point accordingly. Many entry points have a sandy bottom that spills over into plains of flowing soft corals.

Look for burrowing creatures in the sandy bottom, including the blind shrimp and the alert goby, whose symbiotic teamwork is a fascinating study in inter-

Location: Northeast Menjangan Island

Depth Range: 3-40m (10-130ft)

Access: Boat

Expertise Rating: Novice

dependency. Watch how the shrimp's antennae constantly touch one of the goby's fins. A flick of the fin warns the shrimp of impending danger. The goby's alertness earns it a safe and constantly bulldozed hole. If threatened, both creatures disappear to safety.

You'll find bommies and some sponge life along the gradual slope. Though sea fans and unique invertebrate life cover the wall and drop-off, this dive does not have the abundant and beautiful wall corals of Menjangan's southern side.

Coral Gardens is especially appropriate for newer divers and snorkelers. There are a number of soft corals in the shallows and lots of small chromis and reef fish. Shells, nudibranchs and various anemones are also easily seen in the shallows.

Maiden gobies burrow into the sandy bottom.

7 Anker Wreck

Due to a lack of official historical sources, there is much speculation about the origins of this wood and copper shipwreck. Some believe that it was a Dutch ship built in the late 1800s and sunk during WWII. Other theorists say it was a slave ship and went down much earlier than that. One thing is for sure: It has been underwater for a long time.

Location: Northwest Menjangan Island

Depth Range: 5.5-40m+ (18-130ft+)

Access: Boat

Expertise Rating: Advanced

Few people get to dive a wreck this old, so it is a unique log entry. Similar old vessels—with copper siding riveted to a wooden rib cage—lie in various stages of decay all over the Indo-Pacific. This one isn't in bad shape, though it is mostly collapsed and impenetrable. The encrusting corals and invertebrates that smother it have helped to preserve its shape.

A shallow mooring buoy marks the site of the wreck's namesake anchor, though there is quite a bit more worth seeing. Some of the wreck is within safe diving depths, but the best parts are at or beyond recreational diving limits. Keep a close eye on your gauges.

The anchor rests at 5.5m along a steep slope. From here, descend along the nicely adorned slope to the first pieces of the wreck at about 27m. You won't find much protection from the

Dense sessile marine life decorates the Anker Wreck.

currents, which are typical here, so be careful not to damage marine life. If the currents seem too strong, just turn the dive into a drift and save the wreck for slack tide.

The slope flattens out at about 37m and the majority of the ship is scattered diagonally in 40m or so. If you don't immediately see the wreck, look for the schooling surgeonfish feeding in the blue water above the vessel. There's lots of fish action around it, with reef sharks, many kinds of fusiliers, schooling gray snappers and large, hungry-looking bull jacks adding to the mix.

Look near the twisted copper siding for strange creatures and unique formations. Along the sloping wall, you'll find two round porthole-like pieces adorned with soft corals, fan corals, sponges and crinoids. Look for the portions of what appears to be a mast ladder on the wreck itself. Though bottles and some other artifacts have been taken, other heavily encrusted objects still adorn the wreck. The site is within the marine reserve and should not be pilfered.

Moray eels, sea anemones, soft corals and large nudibranchs occupy the reef-top (at 4 to 8m). This wall can get quite steep in places. In others, you'll find canyons and crevices. Although you can continue a deep dive here, after diving the wreck it is safer to cruise at 12 or 15m to see the most colorful corals. Watch your safety-stop time closely.

Living Fossils

Feather stars (also called crinoids) are the most ancient of living echinoderms. They are often found in narrow crevices with only their arms visible, or high atop coral heads, sponges and sea fans. They have small, flat pentagonal bodies with five arms that fork one or more times. Multiple short appendages extend along both sides of each arm, like the quill and vanes of a feather. These pinnate arms are used to filter water for particles of food.

Several species of feather stars are abundant throughout Bali. Many have incredible color combinations and patterns that range from the brightest of yellows to subtle combinations of cream and burgundy. With more than 90 species, Bali has one of the highest concentrations and diversity of crinoids in the world. You'll find them on virtually every reef.

Crinoids have symbiotic relationships with many small sea animals. Look for well-camouflaged clingfish, squat lobster, shrimp and ghost pipefish, which use the crinoids for protection and habitat.

8 Eel Gardens

This reef area has some of the brightest white sand in Indonesia, dotted with large coral heads adorned like Medusa at Mardi Gras. Dives here can be long and relaxed because the bottom rarely dips below 18m. Look around the coral heads for small invertebrate life such as tunicate colonies, which come in a variety of shapes, sizes and colors. Divers usually do a drift dive around the southwest point to the start of Coral Towers. You'll pass through varied terrain, including channels with eagle rays, mantas and, occasionally, dolphins.

Fields of garden eels can be found in the sandy flats here. These small eels feed in the currents in a motion reminiscent of a snake charmer's cobra. When approached, the colony disappears en masse into small burrows in the sand. Look closely and move slowly—it is easy to swim over hundreds and miss them all.

The sponge life is diverse and quite colorful throughout this site. Take a close

Location: West Menjangan Island

Depth Range: 3-18m (10-60ft)

Access: Boat

Expertise Rating: Novice

look at the immense, bright orange elephant ear sponge that reaches more than 2m high. Lots of tunicates grow on the side that faces the current.

Watch for extremely large star pufferfish here, some of which grow to more than a half-meter long. They like to munch on starfish.

Batfish may follow you for most of the dive hoping for a handout, an indication that dive guides have probably fed them in the past. Fish-feeding is discouraged, as it causes fish to change their behavior—they may become dependent and even aggressive.

Garden eels vie for food carried by the interisland current that runs along Eel Garden's sandy bottom.

9 Mimpi Bay

The small and understated yet opulent Mimpi Menjangan Resort sits along a mangrove-lined bay on the Bali coast on the national park's eastern edge. The resort has natural hot springs and a dive center complete with boats and a training pool. It has also discovered a series of dives suitable for those who want to see something a little different from the Menjangan Island dive sites. Macrophotographers are continually finding new areas to work.

As you head out toward the channel mouth, you'll come to **Mimpi Lagoon**, a site on a sandy and occasionally muddy slope that dips from 1 to 12m. Look for a variety of nudibranchs, gobies, ghost pipefish and even frogfish in the sand and coral rubble.

Location: Mimpi Menjangan Beach

Depth Range: 1-27m (3-90ft)

Access: Boat

Expertise Rating: Novice

Mimpi Tunnel is the channel between the bay and the sea. Watch out for currents here when the tide is changing. The tunnel leads to an outer wall that drops from 4.5 to 35m. The wall is alive with small fish and fan corals. Look for dolphin pods, usually seen at the surface near the mouth of the channel, as well as schools of jumping albacore tuna.

A right turn as you exit the channel takes you to **Mimpi Point**, an extension of this wall and a favorite site for night dives. Since Menjangan Island is closed to divers at night, this satisfies those who want a night-diving fix. This site also has a drop-off with soft corals and gorgonians and is a good place to see sea snakes.

Your chances of seeing eagle rays are pretty good at **Sandy Point**, just northwest of the bay. This is an extremely productive site for finding lacy ghost pipefish. Many kinds of schooling fish sometimes cruise by the point. Be aware of the possible current here.

Mimpi Bay and the outer reef of Mimpi Lagoon may produce many

The ghost pipefish is one of the most sought-after creatures for fish lovers to observe and photograph.

surprises in the coming years as guests and divemasters continue to explore the area. Both a sailfish and a dolphin have wandered into the mangrove-lined waters, much to the surprise of residents. Tuna, schools of juvenile barracuda and other colorful juvenile fish have also been seen here, so ask the guides if any unusual marine action is taking place.

10 | Secret Bay

The secret is out! This little backwater bay opposite the ferry dock near Gilimanuk's commercial port has some of the strangest creatures in the sea. This dive site was discovered by Takamasa Tonozuka, one of Bali's most knowledgeable marine experts and underwater photographers, who sought a dive site with rare and unusual life. Secret Bay definitely fits the bill.

Location: Teluk Gilimanuk

Depth Range: 0-10m (0-33ft)

Access: Shore

Expertise Rating: Novice

Its calm, shallow and clear waters are a delight for anyone interested in learning about marine life. The bay's rare and abundant critters make it a mecca for serious macrophotographers.

The easy shore entry and shallow depth make Secret Bay ideal for novice divers.

The cold current that feeds this bay seems to be of part what attracts these critters, so you will want to bring a 3m wetsuit as most divers get cold by the end of this long, shallow dive. If you can catch a morning high tide, visibility should be good.

The walk-in shore entry is in front of Dive & Dive's Secret Bay dive shop, which provides small but comfortable rooms as well as a changing area, spacious gearing-up area, showers, camera table and rinse tanks. There are also some lounge chairs on the nicely manicured grounds, so divers can warm up by catching some rays between dives.

A seahorse's silhouette is a striking photo subject.

Things start happening almost immediately upon submersion. Clumps of seagrass host camouflaged pipefish, fire urchins and tassled filefish. It seems that every fin kick brings something new into view. Odd bristleworms eat a jellyfish and then disappear into the sand. Red and yellow seahorses (ranging from 7 to 15cm long) blend in with plant life. Small cuttlefish hug the bottom.

Look for Cassiopea jellyfish, juvenile lionfish and scorpionfish, very odd and colorful flatworms, pleurobranchs, nudibranchs, eel-like hairtail blennies swimming in the open, tiger-stripe pipefish, batfish and sea cucumbers in weed stands, cockatoo leaf fish, sleeping striped puffers, schools of milkfish, sand crabs, decorator crabs with various anemones, weedy scorpionfish, ambon scorpionfish—the list goes on. This is just in the daytime!

In the evening, mandarinfish, mimic octopuses, frogfish and a whole new list of creatures venture out. You'll find all this life in less than 10m of water.

You can hire a dive guide for only a few U.S. dollars. This is highly recommended, as a guide's trained eyes can pick out hard-to-see creatures, such as delicate ghost pipefish. Most divers would otherwise swim right by this fish, mistaking it for a piece of seaweed.

It is not hard to see that this bay is filled with trash. However, a trash cleanup was undertaken once and many of the unique creatures disappeared. The "junk" on the bottom provides a habitat for this odd clutch of fish.

Pemuteran Dive Sites

The small village of Pemuteran has developed into a beachfront resort area nestled up against the dramatic foothills of the Taman Nasional Bali Barat. The region can be dived as a daytrip from Kuta (about a four-hour drive) or from Lovina (90 minutes east), but Pemuteran has become a destination in its own right. The pleasant accommodations make at least an overnight trip a sensible option. The few local hotels can organize hikes for those who want to explore the area on foot. Several dive shops now service the region, offering local dives and trips to Menjangan Island and destinations as far away as Tulamben.

Reef Seen, the region's oldest dive shop, scouted out most of the local dive sites and has been a pioneer of education and conservation practices. The shop has helped locals and visitors to value the marine habitat—the condition of the reefs has improved as a result of changed behaviors and practices. Nothing can be taken from the reefs except pictures. Dynamite fishing and indiscriminate aquarium-fish collecting was largely eliminated in the early '90s, and the

Hatch & Release

In traditional Balinese religion, the island is believed to ride on the back of a giant turtle god. Ironically, the sea turtle is also considered a delicacy in Bali. Laws limit the number and size of turtles that can be caught per year, and bylaws restrict their use and consumption to religious and cultural ceremonies. Despite this, Bali continues to be the center of the illicit Indonesian turtle trade. Consequently, the region's turtle population is endangered, and turtle populations continue to decline worldwide.

In order to conserve the precious sea turtle, Pemuteran's Reef Seen has established the Proyek Penyu (Turtle Project), a nonprofit sea-turtle hatchery. Green and hawksbill sea turtles are hatched, then released into the wild when they are able to fend for themselves. Older turtles and eggs are purchased to promote the survival of these aquatic reptiles. You can visit Reef Seen's tanks to see the baby turtles, and are welcome to sponsor a baby or make a donation to help this worthy cause.

Snorkeling with a hawksbill hatchling.

region's turtle population is increasing because of Reef Seen's turtle hatchery and protection program.

Pemuteran Bay is usually calm and dive sites are all less than 20 minutes from shore. Most reefs have gentle slopes that feature lots of hard corals and fish action on the top. Sea fans, soft corals, giant sponges, schooling fish and pelagics are seen in the deeper, current-fed reaches. Most of the sites are appropriate for all divers and have a variety of marine life—from the occasional manta ray and whale shark to the elusive leaf scorpionfish and seahorse. You can do night dives and long, shallow dives right from shore.

Look for whale sharks in deeper waters.

The area is recovering from the effects of 1997's El Niño conditions. Though some sites are still blighted at reeftop, coral-rich deeper areas attract fish and occasional pelagics. Divemasters continue to explore the area for new reefs, so ask about any recent discoveries.

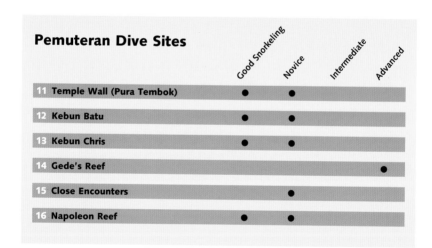

Pemuteran Dive Sites

	Good Snorkeling	Novice	Intermediate	Advanced
11 Temple Wall (Pura Tembok)	●	●		
12 Kebun Batu	●	●		
13 Kebun Chris	●	●		
14 Gede's Reef				●
15 Close Encounters			●	
16 Napoleon Reef	●	●		

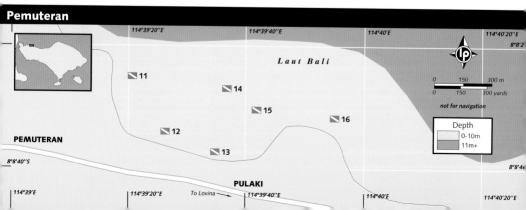

Pemuteran

11 Temple Wall (Pura Tembok)

You'll find this wall dive in front of a Balinese hilltop temple that overlooks Pemuteran Bay. From the temple, the Bali sun rises on one side and the cloud-covered volcanoes of eastern Java spread out on the other.

Underwater, this wall is full of surprises. It starts in shallow water (3m or less depending on the tide) and drops below 27m in some places. The wall gives way to a sandy bottom with scattered hard-coral heads adorned with sea fans and the ever-present barrel sponges.

Small lobster, varied nudibranchs, flatworms and pipefish are abundant on this reef. Silt is a little heavy here, but it benefits the sea fan population by providing a ready food source. Varied sponge life, black corals, wild wire corals and sea fans beautifully adorn the reef's small crevices and pockets. Other invertebrates, including scalloped oysters, are found along this series of cuts and overhangs. Layered sea fans shelter lionfish, small baitfish and brilliant damselfish.

Location: Pemuteran Bay

Depth Range: 4.6-30m (15-100ft)

Access: Boat

Expertise Rating: Novice

You'll find various coral species growing in the shallow water, such as the large razor coral found along the sandy rubble. Napoleon wrasses and jacks come here to forage amid the scattered coral heads. Small flatworms and reef fish hang out around the large bommies. This is also a good place to find critters like eggshell cowries and an occasional fluted oyster.

The profuse invertebrate life makes Temple Wall an excellent night dive. After dark, all kinds of creatures come out or unfold, creating an incredible explosion of color everywhere the diver's light points. Look for basket stars and amazing crinoids.

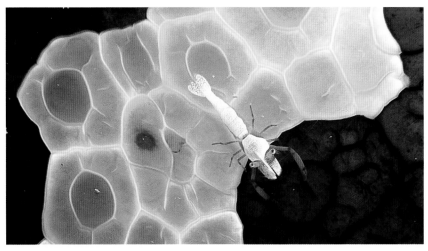

The unusual pluerobranch and its accompanying commensal shrimp can be seen here at night.

12 Kebun Batu

Kebun Batu, which means Rock Gardens, can be reached from the Reef Seen beach. By day this is a pretty drop-off with cabbage corals growing one atop the other, creating a beautiful layered effect.

Location: Pemuteran Bay

Depth Range: 3-24m (10-80ft)

Access: Shore or boat

Expertise Rating: Novice

By night this dive is great, especially if you're into small and unusual invertebrates. Along a walled coral head that drops to about 15m, camouflage spider crabs that resemble debris blend into the background of an ascidian-covered orange sponge. Shrimp, slipper lobster, tiny hermit crabs and large reef crabs are all prolific. Also, look for the prehistoric-looking spongehead crab (a large crab that has adopted a half-meter sponge) and the Neanderthal spider crab (which resembles something built by Mother Nature's erector set gone awry).

Look amid the cabbage corals for ringed pipefish with dazzling red and white markings. At this site, you may see large pleurobranchs—animals similar to nudibranchs but without the flowing gills. Their unique patterns and accompanying shrimp make them great abstract photography subjects. Add some unusual tube worms, feather duster worms and a large purple-tipped sea anemone with brilliant orange clown anemonefish (all found in only 3m of water) and you have hours of pleasurable snorkeling or diving.

A diver illuminates an anemone's tentacles.

13 Kebun Chris

If you want a good look at Indo-Pacific invertebrates, be sure to check out this shallow reef just a short swim from the beach right in front of the Reef Seen aquatic center. It is good for snorkeling, an introductory dive, a shallow last dive of the day or a long and leisurely night dive.

Location: Pemuteran Bay

Depth Range: 3-18m (6-60ft)

Access: Shore or boat

Expertise Rating: Novice

The reef at Kebun Chris, which means Chris' Garden, gradually slopes down to 18m. Various porites and acropora corals make up the bulk of the coral growth here.

At night, crinoids extend from the tops of the coral heads to catch food in the current. They make excellent macrophotography subjects. Beautiful anemone hermit crabs scour the sandy seafloor looking for a morsel to eat, their shells covered with dazzling white sea anemones. You'll also see a variety of eels, glass shrimp and cleaner shrimp, crabs and nudibranchs on the reef after dark. At least four different species of pipefish reside here. Small sea pens (just 5cm long) grow from the sand right under the boat anchorage. They come out only at night.

Juvenile cardinalfish, stonefish and lionfish conceal themselves along the coral heads. They make great macrophotography subjects because they fit well into a framer and are usually so stunned by a diver's light that they will hold still long enough for you to take a photo. Look out for their dorsal spines, however. Though small, they can inflict a painful wound.

Part of the reef is regrowing after being damaged first by storm waves many years ago and then again by the late-'90s El Niño conditions. Be careful not to dislodge the new corals and sponges that are trying to rebuild in the rubble.

This nudibranch has laid a ribbon of eggs.

Aquatic Equestrians

In Pemuteran's waters, you may see a unique seahorse species—of the equestrian variety. The horses from Reef Seen's stables are often taken into the sea for a soothing swim.

Snorkeling with one of these "sea horses" can be a fun and unique experience.

Horseback riding along a number of trails is also available. You can ride off into the fading sun, around the point and along the edge of a beautiful, undeveloped bay. The rugged hills, with their peaks sometimes shrouded by clouds, loom ahead as you ride beside jungle and forest, through rural villages and homesteads, past doe-eyed cattle and down into the valley. The chance to see some bird life, deer and even a Bali anteater makes this a great gallop for the nature lover.

Tours are slated for early morning or late afternoon to take advantage of cooler temperatures and less-intense sun. While some of the horses are quite spirited, newer riders will find ones with calmer dispositions. Taking a ride along the beach or into the hills can be a pleasant way to see the terrain and is a great break if you're getting "dived out."

14 Gede's Reef

You can reach Gede's Reef after a 20-minute boat ride along the Pemuteran coast. It is worth the trip if you like beautiful sponges, sea fans and hard corals. The silhouetted triple volcanoes of Java to the west lend an exotic air to this dive site.

The reef is shaped roughly like an 8. The north end, called **Rock's Point**, is in 25 to 30m of water. It is home to sea fans, black-coral trees and sponges. Look for lionfish, including feathery black *pterois* juveniles, which tend to be solitary and secretive. You'll see anemones along the bottom and brittle stars attached to sea fans.

It may be worth your while to search for pygmy seahorses amid the *Muricella*

Location: Pemuteran Bay

Depth Range: 14-40m (45-130ft)

Access: Boat

Expertise Rating: Advanced

sea fans here, especially when the cooler upwellings come through in September and October. These tiny seahorses haven't been seen in this part of Bali yet, but they have been confirmed in the Tulamben area. Given the abundance of their favorite habitat, it stands to reason that they are here as well.

The east end of the sloping reef rises in a steep bank to 15m and is covered with the bay's best hard-coral growth. Huge cabbage corals, gardens of vase and tube sponges, and other porites coral species grow in wild and beautiful formations.

The current over the east end brings plenty of nutrients to the reef, setting the stage for fish-watching by attracting a variety of species. Small schools of jacks and fusiliers come in from out of the blue. At the reeftop look for cuttlefish, which flash wild colors while heading toward their prey. In the upper areas at around 18m, garden outcrops of tube sponges, carpets of smaller sponges and soft corals combine to create an oasis of seascaped beauty.

15 Close Encounters

Lucky divers may have a close encounter with the manta rays that occasionally traverse this dive site. One of the mantas is pure white, making for an unearthly experience with these gentle and graceful creatures.

Many large occupants frequent this totally unpredictable dive site. Whale sharks are sometimes seen here between December and April (when the plankton is most abundant) but can appear at any time. Potato cod (an enormous and fairly rare type of grouper) as well as Napoleon wrasses, king mackerel, large tuna and grey reef sharks visit this site. Even whales have been seen spouting very close to dive boats in the area.

You'll see large coral heads and abundant fish life all over the reef. Big bumphead parrotfish are occasionally observed chomping on coral at the southwest end of the reef. Huge sponges, bigger than an easy chair, are the norm here. Don't be fooled by the well-

Location: Pemuteran Bay

Depth Range: 7.6-40m (25-130ft)

Access: Boat

Expertise Rating: Novice

camouflaged leaf fish, which sway in the surge like actual pieces of fallen flora.

A small channel reef splits off from the east end of the main reef. It has a great fish population and some healthy hard corals and gorgonians.

A close encounter with a manta can be an unearthly experience.

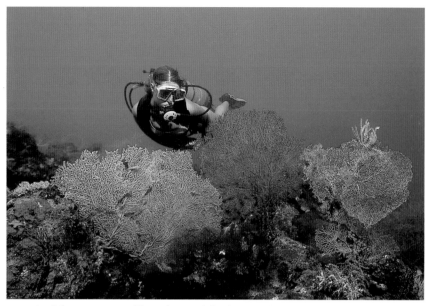

Look for macro marine life residing amid the dense coral growth at Close Encounters.

Also at this end of the main reef, you'll see garden eels protruding from their homes in the seafloor, picking nutrients from the current as they sway gently to and fro. Divers must approach the eels slowly and breathe very lightly, as quick movements and bubbles will cause them to disappear into the sand.

16 Napoleon Reef

Named for a large Napoleon wrasse seen here regularly, this great little reef has it all. It can be dived deep or shallow, day or night. On the northeast end of the reef is the *ikan warung*, or fish house, where you'll see schools of fish all over the place. Golden sea fans and large clumps of cotton-candy coral grow beside other gorgonians along the slope.

Take a turn around the east end of the reef and head south, where you'll find large barrel sponges that are more than 1.5m high and 1m in diameter. Crinoids cling to their outer edges, while damsels sometimes hover inside. The sea fans and cotton-candy corals house pairs of fantail pipefish, cardinalfish and small

Location: Pemuteran Bay

Depth Range: 4.6-40m (15-130ft)

Access: Boat

Expertise Rating: Novice

damselfish. Cleaning stations are positioned along the southern edge of the reef, where you'll see colorful Pederson shrimp sitting amid the wavy hard corals and the anemonelike tentacles of mushroom coral.

The coral gardens along this rich reef's shallow areas were once spectacular, but are now recovering from a dreadful bout with El Niño. The water temperatures here were above 31°C for three months in 1997, and most of the upper reef corals took a bad hit. There are exceptions. A few healthy stands of castle porites attract swarms of small fish and a school of copper sweepers.

This reef is an ideal location to observe cuttlefish and their egg-laying behavior. Normally wary of divers, cuttlefish aren't easily distracted from planting their eggs in the protective branches of fire coral. You'll see cuttlefish here, especially in the late afternoons, and can watch them for a long time, as the coral is shallow. The large platter corals growing one atop the other formed a beautiful layered scene prior to El Niño. These clumps of coral may have dozens of small egg sacs deposited deep within their branches. Cuttlefish approach the coral and extend their long tentacles like a funnel. The fish then lays a small, soft egg sac and attaches it to the coral. Cuttlefish can do this for hours, until the inner branches of the coral head are filled with eggs.

The platter corals are at only 6m and can be snorkeled as well as dived. Be aware that a current runs over the top here when the tide is changing. Bright yellow trumpetfish tailed by similarly colored jacks feed in the light current—the fish use each other as an odd form of camouflage. Joining them are grey snappers, yellowspot jacks, rainbow runners and an occasional barracuda, as well as myriad chromis and basslets. Large fusilier schools and a variety of sea stars are commonly seen on this dive.

Gone in a Flash

Cuttlefish, octopus and squid can protect themselves from predators in a variety of ways. These unique reef critters (all members of the cephalopod class) live in water ranging from 6 to 12m (20 to 40ft) deep. These unique reef critters can protect themselves from predators in a variety of ways. Cephalopods, among the most advanced of all invertebrates, can maneuver better than most sea animals. They expel a stream of water from a small siphon that can be pointed in any direction, allowing them to propel themselves, sometimes at blinding speed.

But this jet propulsion system isn't the only way cephalopods avoid becoming someone's meal. In the blink of an eye, they can expertly blend in with their surroundings. Their chromatophores—color pigments controlled by radial muscles in cephalopods' unique dual (local and central) nervous system—expand and contract, creating an amazing Technicolor light show. They have the most powerful neurological system known to science, and their ability to quickly camouflage themselves is unrivaled in the animal world. They can also change color when curious, amorous, alarmed or showing aggression. Cephalopods tend to be territorial, so once you see one you can return to the same site and will likely see it again.

Tulamben Dive Sites

Daytrippers traveling from Kuta to the east Bali dive regions of Tulamben and Amed will get a look at traditional Balinese cities and attractive rural settings. Get an early-morning start out of the touristed city areas and head into the rural countryside. The Balinese rise early, around 5am, and everything happens on the street, so villages you'll pass along the way are a flurry of activity. The road winds through beautifully terraced rice paddies, past the majestic volcano Gunung Agung and through badlands of towering pandanas trees. The sights, sounds and smells provide a look into Indonesian daily life and help pass the time on the three-hour trip from Kuta. The drive is considerably shorter if you stay outside of Kuta: 90 minutes from Candidasa, an hour from Tirta Gangga, two from Lovina and three from Pemuteran.

The road skirts the coastline and passes through the small village of Tulamben, where equipment porters of all ages and sizes seem to come out of nowhere as soon as you stop here. Unless you drove on your own and brought everything with you, your dive operator will prearrange to have the porters transport your gear to the dive site. All you have to do is wander down to the beach. A short walk past multicolored outriggers will bring you to a black, rocky beach.

Diving in Tulamben is normally done from shore, where the entry is usually easy albeit slightly tricky. Though the rocky bottom near shore isn't slippery, the rocks do move a little with the surf and your weight, so don't be hasty when wading into

Resilient Tulamben Porters

The rugged volcanic rock of Tulamben's beaches can make a short walk to the dive site seem interminable. Not to worry: A group composed mainly of Tulamben village women has organized a porter cooperative, offering divers a much-appreciated service. This hard work raises money for both the community and the women's households. Porters will carry your diving equipment to the dive site, and greet you at water's edge after your dive to carry the equipment back. Their fee is already included in your dive package. You might as well let them do it, because you're charged whether they carry it or not.

The porters carry the gear (tank and all) on their heads! If that's not amazing enough, these enterprising women sometimes heft two or even three tanks at the same time. Plus, they'll have weight belts hanging over their shoulders. Armed with only flip-flops on their feet and their own amazing strength, they can brave even the roughest of conditions, able to deliver the equipment safe and sound. Take time to talk to them if you can, as they're lovely company and are always up for a joke or a song.

—by Susanna Hinderks

the sea. Move out to thigh-level water, inflate your BC and float while putting on your fins. Then look down. The vibrant reef colors stand out against the sloping black sand.

Many people prefer to stay in Tulamben rather than drive here for a daytrip. A number of fun restaurants and small hotels make an overnight stay comfortable. Local, Western and European cuisine can be found at reasonable prices along the short Tulamben strip. Most hotels have little seaside eateries where you can watch the moon rise over the bay. The quiet star-filled evenings punctuated only by the sound of the surf are a perfect escape from Kuta madness. The local people are very friendly, so you'll have a chance to interact with these gregarious Balinese.

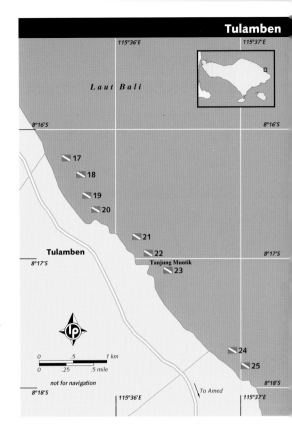

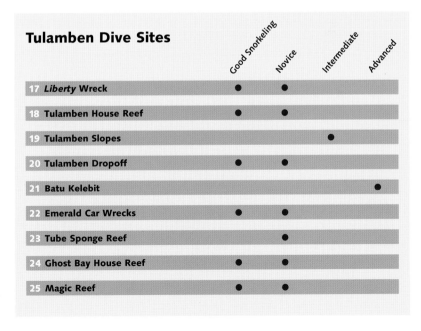

Tulamben Dive Sites	Good Snorkeling	Novice	Intermediate	Advanced
17 *Liberty* Wreck	●	●		
18 Tulamben House Reef	●	●		
19 Tulamben Slopes			●	
20 Tulamben Dropoff	●	●		
21 Batu Kelebit				●
22 Emerald Car Wrecks	●	●		
23 Tube Sponge Reef		●		
24 Ghost Bay House Reef	●	●		
25 Magic Reef	●	●		

17 *Liberty* Wreck

The American ship USAT *Liberty* is Bali's most popular and accessible dive. This large war victim is the island's most intact divable wreck and is just a two-minute swim from shore. Many divers make the pilgrimage to Tulamben to see her. Others stay in the village to make repeat dives and become better acquainted with her dazzling corals and fish life.

Location: Tulamben Bay

Depth Range: 3-37m (10-120ft)

Access: Shore

Expertise Rating: Novice

This armed cargo ship (not a Liberty-class vessel) was built in 1915 and served as a supply ship during WWII. A Japanese submarine torpedoed her on January 11, 1942, while she was in the strait about ten miles southwest of Lombok. Two destroyers, the HMNS *Van Ghent* and the USS *Paul Jones,* came to her rescue and towed her toward Bali.

Her damage was extensive, so the crew was evacuated and she was purposely beached. The Americans intended to return and salvage her contents (raw rubber and railroad parts, among other things), but the war escalated and that never happened. The intact ship sat beached on this pristine coast until Bali's volcanic Gunung Agung blew its stack in 1963. The *Liberty* toppled beneath the water during that extremely violent eruption.

Black coral grows inside the *Liberty*'s hold.

Liberty wreck diver examines apricot fan coral.

This large and somewhat broken-up wreck now sits on a black-sand shelf that slopes from about 6 to 37m. She is a big wreck, perhaps 120m long, and lies parallel to the beach with her bow pointing north. The stern is somewhat intact, the midships in shambles and the bow in pretty good shape.

The wreck's years under the sea have been good for divers. The *Liberty* has become one of Indonesia's most beautiful artificial reefs and is nicer than many natural reefs as well. The currents running by the wreck bring lots of nutrients to feed the corals, magnificent gorgonian

Wreck Diving

Wreck diving can be safe and fascinating. Penetration of shipwrecks, however, is a skilled specialty and should not be attempted without proper training. Wrecks are often unstable; they can be silty, deep and disorienting. Use an experienced guide to view wrecks and the amazing coral communities that have developed on them.

sea fans, huge soft-coral trees and big barrel sponges that flourish here.

The largest concentrations of huge gorgonians, sponges and corals are around the stern and stern gun and at midships near the catwalks of the engine room. Look for anemones and nudibranchs in the coral-encrusted areas. The corals here are fragile—please be careful with your fins and avoid touching any marine life so as not to do any damage.

A resident school of bigeye jacks lives on and around the ship. Look for them especially in the bow area. These fish are unafraid of divers, so it is safe and fun to enter the school and have them whirl around you. The ship is also a haven for a variety of large angelfish, batfish, sweetlips and parrotfish.

Night diving on the *Liberty* is popular. The soft corals and tubastrea are dazzling after the sun goes down. Look for sleeping fish and lots of invertebrates, especially nudibranchs and flatworms, crawling around at night. Divers commonly see schooling flashlight fish—the fireflies of the sea—near midships where the head areas meet the sand.

A word of warning is in order: There are still some passages and rooms that can be entered, but the ship continues to deteriorate, and as it does, sections collapse. It is best to avoid penetration and do only overswims of this famous wreck.

18 Tulamben House Reef

You'll need to slow down a bit to see everything Tulamben House Reef has to offer. Situated in front of the Paradise Restaurant, this mass of low-growing corals, sponges and anemones is one of the most fascinating little stretches of ocean in Bali.

The reef is known for its diversity of fish life, with at least 300 species living in this compact area. Most impressive are the big, schooling bumphead parrotfish that graze here almost daily. Look for them at morning high tide.

Location: Tulamben Bay

Depth Range: 1.8-15m (6-50ft)

Access: Shore

Expertise Rating: Novice

There are other odd creatures like ribbon eels, leaf fish, a variety of triggerfish, many species of parrotfish, cleaning stations where big groupers and striped sweetlips line up, tridacna clams, oriental sweetlips, mating octopuses and sometimes cuttlefish laying eggs. And that list just scratches the surface.

You can see at least five different anemone species accompanied by spinecheeks, perculas, saddlebacks and skunk clownfish. Porcelain crabs and shrimp also hide in the anemones' tentacles.

This shallow reef has lots of cracks and crevices for invertebrates to seek refuge in, making it a great night dive. Mantis shrimp come out of their holes. Many kinds of stonefish, scorpionfish and even the odd devilfish can be seen on the prowl. Nudibranchs and sleeping fish are common. The reef is shallow and close to shore, so divers can enjoy long dives and see lots of marine life.

Though El Niño changed the face of this reef, it is mostly intact and marine life remains abundant. It is especially nice at sunrise and just before sunset, when the fish are most active.

Saddlebacks hover around an anemone host.

19   Tulamben Slopes

If you are in Tulamben on a daytrip, it's worth making this one of the day's two dives. These black-sand slopes are some of the richest in the world. Tulamben Slopes—encompassing the area between House Reef and Tulamben Dropoff—is especially popular with biologists and underwater photo pros. Here you can see a diversity of invertebrates, find unusual fish and observe unique marine-life behavior.

Location: Tulamben Bay

Depth Range: 7.6-40m (25-130ft)

Access: Shore

Expertise Rating: Intermediate

The slopes are littered with a few rocks, barrel sponges and the odd coral head but, in fact, really don't look like much. However, take the time to look closely and an amazing and delicate world will be revealed. The rocks are home to white-eyed moray eels, long-beak shrimp, lionfish and stonefish. Crinoids—with harlequin ghost pipefish nestled amid their feathery arms—may also be found on these rocks. The crinoids often conceal a squat lobster, a clingfish or glass shrimp. Symbiotic relationships are formed with seemingly wild abandon here.

Each little rock and coral colony is an oasis of macro invertebrate life. Look for mantis shrimp, nudibranchs and sand anemones popping up out of the seafloor. You may see pastel yellow and brilliant orange sea pens as they emerge from the substrate.

The fish life is also notable. A few resident barracuda roam the sandy slopes, milkfish flourish in the shallows and bull jacks cruise the reef in search of prey.

Watch your time and depth here. It is easy to lose track as you explore the rolling undersea hills, especially when there's activity at the many cleaning stations. Night dives here can also be rewarding, with invertebrates emerging from the reef. Also, look for barracuda and whitetip reef sharks lurking at your dive light's edge.

The hairy crab is a rare find that is known to live on barrel sponges here and at the Dropoff.

20 | Tulamben Dropoff

Divers gear up for this dive at the south end of Tulamben Bay. You can walk in and swim along the black-sand slope, then head out east to the corner where rocks protrude from the water just off the point. Here, basslets glitter over the reef-top and small gorgonians sway in the gentle surge. After a short swim, the sheer wall of the drop-off comes into view and the sea life increases with every fin kick.

The current at the point attracts lots of fish, which you'll see in the open water as you swim along the wall. The wall itself is a seascape of colorful sponge life and coral growth.

At 30m, the current usually flows south around the first finger of the point, where a Tulamben landmark, a huge red *Muricella* sea fan, comes into view. Appearing dark violet at this depth, the fan is a remarkable sight—even the most jaded diver will admire its size and intricacy. Those with an eye for detail may spot a tiny, rare pygmy seahorse on the sea fans in this area. The fan hosts many other fish as well, including hawkfish.

Location: Tulamben Bay

Depth Range: 6.1-40m (20-130ft)

Access: Shore

Expertise Rating: Novice

The probability is high that some pelagic action will add a thrill to your dives here. Keep an eye on the blue water for whale sharks, manta rays, hammerheads, mola-molas, sharks and dogtooth tuna. They are attracted to the plankton carried by the current that sweeps in from the Tulamben Slopes.

Perhaps the most striking aspect of the shallows are the huge sponges. Big barrel sponges and stands of purple tube sponges add form and color to an already bustling reef. Keep an eye out for unusual, spiny electric-pink and

Sponge Spawn

Bali has abundant barrel sponges, some growing to the size of easy chairs, on most of its reefs. Divers fortunate enough to witness the spawn of one of these behemoths will see the water become suddenly filled by the simultaneous release of sperm and eggs. It is presumed that this spawning behavior is triggered by the lunar cycle. It is not unusual to see large snappers and other smaller fish gather to ingest this release. Barrel sponges, members of the *Xestospongia* family, provide homes to a huge variety of animals including shrimp, crabs, worms, barnacles, holthurians (small sea cucumbers) and fish.

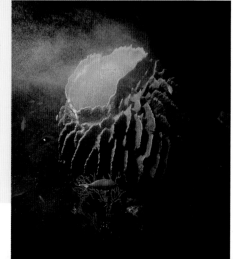

neon-violet squat lobsters within the folds of the big barrel sponges. These lobster, *Lauria siagiani*, were first identified by the well-known Bali dive guide Wally Siagian and named in his honor.

Nearby, anemones with Pederson shrimp and clown anemonefish feed in the rich water. Divers usually return over the shallow reaches along the top of the wall where angelfish, spotted groupers and parrotfish thrive.

Come back along the bay's shore in the shallows to extend the dive and see lots of invertebrate life. As you exit the water, you'll see the hillside Hindu temple that stands watch over Tulamben Bay. The temple is dwarfed by the looming, distant Gunung Agung. Visibility can be low at the Dropoff during the rainy season, but the runoff feeds the immense sponges, so it's not a bad trade-off.

While most divers prefer the easier night dives in front of the hotels, this can be a good site for an after-dark romp.

Delicate gorgonian fans make striking photo subjects.

Pygmy Seahorses

Finding a pygmy seahorse has been all the rage for biologists and underwater photographers in recent years. Though they were discovered in 1969, not much was known about their habitat, distribution or behavior until fairly recently.

Seahorses are members of the family *Syngnathidae*, which also includes pipefish, pipehorses and sea dragons. Most seahorses live in shallow coastal waters, areas where human disturbance has become both intensive and extensive. Seahorse habitats, such as seagrass meadows, coral reefs and mangroves, are among the most threatened in the world. Pollution, shoreline alteration and destructive fishing methods such as trawling and dynamite fishing all contribute to habitat degradation that in turn affects seahorses.

Unlike its cousins, the pygmy seahorse usually lives in deep water (below 18m). Specimens have been found in Papua New Guinea waters, in the southern Philippines and in eastern and central Indonesia. The tiny (perhaps 4cm long) *Hippocampus bargibanti* has been found on *Muricella* sea fans along Tulamben's shores (at the *Liberty* wreck and at the Dropoff). Its habitat may extend along the coast to other areas of Bali where these fans flourish.

Finding a pygmy seahorse isn't easy. They are camouflaged to look like the sea fan's polyps and may move around the fan. It is best to use a magnifying glass and scan the sea fan systematically. A good guide who knows what to look for is a major help the first time you try to find one. Pygmy seahorses become stressed easily, so if you come across one, be kind—don't move it.

21   Batu Kelebit

Location: South of Tulamben

Depth Range: 9.1-55m (30-180ft)

Access: Boat

Expertise Rating: Advanced

This sloping mound ends in a series of deep reefs that resemble the top of a seamount. Though the cold currents can be quite strong here, they aren't totally unmanageable. They occur at the surface and down the slope, but tend to dissipate in the deeper reaches.

The reefs at this deep dive fan out into the sand, rising only 3 to 5m from the bottom. They are covered in current-fed hard coral growth featuring acropora and porites species. The striking difference between the white-sand bottom and the array of hard corals makes it unlike anything else in the Tulamben area. Look for resting whitetip sharks and weaving garden eels along the sandy bottom.

Divers often see silky sharks, mantas, mola-molas and other large pelagics here, but most sightings are made well past safe sport-diving limits.

Look also for an array of invertebrates, including yellow-and-black *notordoris* nudibranchs, various sea anemones, *dendrophyllia* soft corals and amazing vase, barrel, rope and maze sponge formations. Branching green tubastrea coral also reaches up from the sandy bottom.

Barrel sponges thrive in the current-swept reaches of Batu Kelebit.

22 Emerald Car Wrecks

Many years ago the large Emerald Tulamben Beach Hotel made an effort to improve the area's diving potential by sinking a pair of cars off its dock, in the snorkeling area south of Batu Kelebit. The cars have developed into an artificial reef despite the environmentally unsound methods used to place the crude cement moorings.

This is now a fun site where divers can see the two autos and their soft-coral cover, which serve as habitat for fish and invertebrates. The soft corals have grown to nice proportions over the years.

Location: South of Tulamben

Depth Range: 3-27m (10-90ft)

Access: Shore or boat

Expertise Rating: Novice

Swim down along the slope from the hotel snorkeling pontoon and head slightly south to see the numerous garden eels that inhabit the white-sand bottom. Batfish greet divers and will

Soft corals sprout from the windows of this scuttled car.

usually stay with you during the course of the dive.

The nearby rocks and the reef south of the cars are home to a varied selection of marine animals. Sea fans and big barrel sponges may have *Lauria siagiani* crabs seeking shelter in their folds. You can finish in the shallows, where the batfish will, no doubt, entertain you during your shallow-water time.

23 Tube Sponge Reef

This little site was found during an exploratory diving trip in the late 1990s. Get someone to take you out on one of the local boats to see what it has to offer—everything from large elephant ear sponges and rope sponges to healthy stands of purple tube sponges. Look for pillow stars on the shallow reef formations, which are dotted with hard corals and sea fans. The ledges at around 15 to 20m are home to lobster, which poke their tentacles out from their lairs. In some crowded holes, lobster cling to the roof and sides of the holes, as well as carpet the bottom.

Location: South of Tulamben

Depth Range: 4.6-30m (15-100ft)

Access: Boat

Expertise Rating: Novice

You can see schooling surgeonfish, butterflyfish and fusiliers playing in the open water. Unfortunately, the abundant fish life has attracted fisherfolk who have left fishing lines entangled in some of the large rock formations and corals.

24 Ghost Bay House Reef

Location: Ghost Bay

Depth Range: 4.6-20m (15-65ft)

Access: Shore or boat

Expertise Rating: Novice

Much of the coast between Tulamben and Amed is still virgin territory, yet to be explored by divers. Ghost Bay—named for its mystical history—is a happy exception. The south end of the bay is held as a holy and sacred place. The bay's central shore is now being developed as a dive resort.

House Reef is a small reef, perhaps 100m long, just offshore. Fortunately, it was largely unaffected by the El Niño conditions and has many healthy corals in just 3 to 14m of water. The setting could not be more perfect for snorkelers, with Gunung Agung clearly visible in the background and colorful rows of jukung fishing boats lining the sandy beach. You can easily see the bluespotted rays, crinoids and hard corals below.

This reef holds many of the tiny creatures for which Tulamben is known. You can see nudibranchs, triggerfish, sea anemones and a host of other invertebrates, including emerald-colored mantis shrimp.

Night diving here is also a promising proposition. Look for flatworms and nudibranchs and be wary of well-camouflaged stonefish.

A mantis shrimp can rotate its compound eyes 360°.

25 Magic Reef

Location: Ghost Bay

Depth Range: 4.6-37m (15-120ft)

Access: Shore or boat

Expertise Rating: Novice

You'll find Magic Reef near the fantastic naturally sculpted volcanic-rock formation at the southeast end of Ghost Bay. Divers gear up in the calm lee of these rocks, then submerge and swim south down the terraced slope.

This reef cascades steeply, but its slope becomes more gradual as it falls in steps to 9, 18 and 27m depths toward the bay's east end. Along the reef's ledges you'll find large barrel sponges, tube sponges and scattered hard corals. Crinoids are present on most of the barrel sponges. Look also for numerous blue-spotted rays resting under the corals and foraging on the slope.

When the current is flowing around the point, look for resident barracuda including yellowtail, barred and the occasional solitary great barracuda. The point's terrain also attracts whitetip reef sharks, surgeonfish and golden-banded butterflyfish schools.

From 12m and up there are small coral bommies with a plethora of anthias and other small tropical fish. Magic Reef is ripe for invertebrate seekers. You'll find unusual nudibranchs in the sand and along the coral bommies. This site also has lots of lionfish and scorpionfish.

One particular highlight that underwater photographers will like is the stunning stand of soft corals north of the reef in about 20m of water. Razorfish do their unusual head-down dance in the billowing arms of these brilliant coral bushes. On the way back up the slope, watch the garden eels.

Blue-spotted rays forage along Magic Reef's slope.

Amed Dive Sites

Amed and the villages southeast of this largely undeveloped scenic area are becoming more popular with tourists. Life here is still slow-paced. To get to Amed, go east at the Culik intersection where the morning market forms, head past the tattoo shop, down through the rice paddies and along the coast where fishing and sea-salt production is still active.

Phone lines haven't yet reached the village, making this an ideal destination for those who want to get away from it all. Small retreats with names like Good Karma

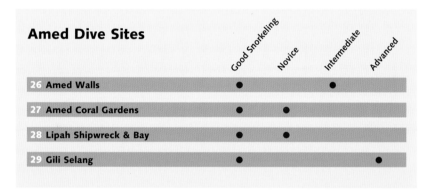

Amed Dive Sites	Good Snorkeling	Novice	Intermediate	Advanced
26 Amed Walls	●		●	
27 Amed Coral Gardens	●	●		
28 Lipah Shipwreck & Bay	●	●		
29 Gili Selang	●			●

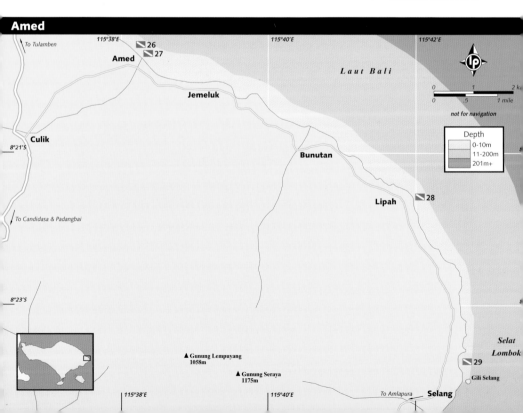

and Reincarnation have sprung up to meet the demand. The area has become a haven for small hotels and dive shops.

Dives are done from local boats and can be arranged right at the shore of Jemeluk Bay. The slow boats don't need to go far to get to the colorful underwater slope, which offers sea fans, large bommies, big sponges, nice drop-offs and diverse fish life. The water here is generally calm most of the year, with currents manageable to minimal. Many sites make excellent drift dives.

26 Amed Walls

Amed has three walls along its most popular stretch of reef, which takes about five minutes to motor out to. The experienced boat drivers will read the current before your dive and put you in at the best spot for a drift dive.

The walls are saddled with the uninspired monikers of **Amed 1**, **Amed 2** and **Amed 3**. There is, however, much to see along the walls and the slopes leading to them. The walls are swept by typically gentle currents and have lots of sea fans, sponges and fish life. Amed 1 is in about 37m to the right of the river channel. Amed 2, directly in front of the channel, is in about 30m. The third wall, Amed 3, is to the left in about 37m.

Divers don't have to go deep to enjoy a dive here. The slope has some barrel and pretzel sponges, big bommies and smaller coral formations. Fish that congregate here include angelfish, Napoleon wrasses, sea turtles and an occasional reef shark at about 28m. You may also see various schools of fish, including sapphire yellowtails and blue-streak fusiliers, which course the reef and occasionally surround divers in a rush of movement and color. Mola-molas have been seen here, normally in the deeper areas where cold upwellings

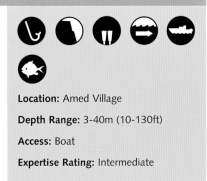

Location: Amed Village

Depth Range: 3-40m (10-130ft)

Access: Boat

Expertise Rating: Intermediate

occur, starting in August and continuing through January.

Red sea whips grow along the walls near Amed.

Moray eels seem to like this spot, perhaps for the abundant fish life that doubles as a meal for the toothy critters. The slope descends to black corals, sponges and some fan corals along the deeper regions of the drop-off. Great clouds of silvery baitfish flit along the overhangs of the central drop-off.

27 Amed Coral Gardens

Though Amed doesn't have the corals that prevail at Bali's eastern dive sites, that doesn't mean this site is sparse. Amed's main attraction is its fish life.

On the southeastern side of this bay, the terrain slopes gradually to a ledge between 9 and 12m. Here you'll find coral heads and fields of staghorn coral interspersed with patches of white sand. These staghorns are home to immense schools of aquarium fish, especially the ever-present anthias and blue-and-silver chromis damsels.

The reef that starts just to the right of the river mouth and runs along the cliffline was once a prime spot for snorkeling, but a combination of El Niño

Location: Amed Village

Depth Range: 3-12m (10-40ft)

Access: Shore or boat

Expertise Rating: Novice

conditions and siltation from upland farms damaged many of the corals in the late '90s. Snorkeling here is still nice but not as colorful as in years past. The fish don't seem to mind, however. For those wanting a shallow dive or snorkel, this is a good spot—you can see a lot in just 5 to 12m.

Butterflyfish (including the brilliant yellow long-nosed butterflyfish), basslets, blennies, chromis and damselfish are just a few of the many fish species you can see in the shallows. Colorful angelfish, including the majestic emperor angelfish and the regal angelfish, are also quite common. Red and golden-yellow gorgonian sea fans adorn the corals, and crinoids are everywhere. Sharks have also been seen sleeping under the platter corals.

This site can make for a good, shallow night dive. Sleeping fish make good photo subjects, and the invertebrate life, including anemone hermit crabs, is active.

Blennies guard the silvery eggs they laid on this tunicate.

28 | Lipah Shipwreck & Bay

The drive to scenic Lipah Bay is one of Bali's true pleasures. This seldom-used narrow coastal road offers dramatic overlooks of Selat Lombok (Lombok Strait) and rural Balinese agricultural scenes in one of the island's most isolated regions.

Location: Lipah Village

Depth Range: 1.8-20m (6-65ft)

Access: Shore or boat

Expertise Rating: Novice

The Lipah Bay wreck is an easy shore dive or snorkel. You can park along the side of the road at the entrance to Lipah village and don your gear. Children will probably gather quickly to watch the spectacle, as not many divers come to this area. The kids will help you navigate the least intrusive way to the shoreline: through tapioca fields, past some cows, around a local house, down a path to the water hole and onto the beach, where dozens of colorful fishing jukungs rest.

A two-minute snorkel slightly southeast from the north shore will bring you to where this wreck of unknown origin rises to just a meter below the surface. The children may stand on the beach and shout directions, so it is hard to miss. This little wreck sits on a sharp slope that falls to about 6m. Its steel hull is adorned in healthy tan soft corals. Plate corals, tunicates and snowy-polyped gorgonians with red skeletons grow along the ship.

The aft ship is fairly open and corals have grown in the ship's ribs. A small helm is also present and somewhat broken. Lots of soft corals adorn the bow, where chromis, anthias and basslets congregate.

This shallow wreck is one of Lipah Bay's many treasures.

The inner bay is mostly sandy with scattered corals and garden eels. Many divers continue out a short distance to the edge of the bay, where the bottom drops off gradually to 18m and then falls abysmally. An assortment of crinoids and reef fish populates the abundant and healthy corals along the drop-off.

The current can be strong on the outer reef at times, so take great care not to get swept away, especially if shore diving. Do this as a drift dive only when there is a boat to pick you up, and always carry a safety sausage with you.

Lipah is near Bali's easternmost point and is not as protected from the trade winds as most other dive regions, so snorkeling or diving here is not always possible. Trade winds pick up in June, so check with local dive experts to get their opinion. But it is a great drive and a fun excursion. Be sure to bring a land camera, as the overlooks of Amed and points south along the road can be stunning.

29 Gili Selang

A small island off Bali's easternmost point, Gili Selang is a good option for divers who are looking for an exciting thrill ride. Check with Amed operators about boat availability and make sure an experienced guide comes along. This can be a tricky dive.

This large rock outcrop is separated from the mainland by a narrow, shallow

Location: Eastern Bali

Depth Range: 4.6-37m (15-120ft)

Access: Boat

Expertise Rating: Advanced

A shallow, narrow channel separates Gili Selang from Bali.

A spotted moray visits a cleaning station at Gili Selang.

channel. Selang sports some green foliage on top, but its bare, rocky east side drops sharply into the open sea facing Lombok. Divers usually enter from in front of the village in the protected eddy near the rock. For those wanting a little action, swim to the outer wall northeast of the island. The brisk current here generally sweeps south.

As you drift near the island's outer face, soft corals increase dramatically and cover the wall in a carpet of eye-popping color. While not large, the orange soft coral and the field of low-growing pink soft corals sway with the flow. If the currents aren't too strong, take a ride at a depth of 18 to 24m along this wall and look for pelagic life. If the currents seem too scary, make your way back before it's too late—it can be difficult or even impossible to turn back. Here's where an experienced guide is invaluable.

This is not a novice dive. Be careful of up- and down-currents. The outgoing currents at the point can carry divers out to sea, so stay to the right and drift into the eddy area behind the rock to finish this ride. This is a convenient place for a safety stop after the more thrilling drift along the wall. On the way, there's a chance you'll see grey reef sharks and whitetip sharks, occasional hammerheads, bumphead parrotfish, big bull jacks, dogtooth tuna and mackerel.

If you're not looking for an adrenaline ride, the bay fronting the village where you make your entry is also a great place to dive. Large eels, big snappers and gorgonian sea fans reside on the big bommies scattered around the bay. It is close to a big fishing village, so it is remarkable there is any marine life in the bay at all. It is a nice dive or snorkel for the fish buffs and macrophotographers who don't crave swift conditions.

Central Coast Dive Sites

Amuk Bay, called Teluk Amuk by the Balinese, is a well-trafficked hour-and-a-half drive northeast of the tourist center of Kuta-Legian. A number of beach towns—Candidasa, Buitan and Padangbai are among the most developed—offer lodging and diving to those wanting some respite from Bali's heavy traffic and tourist hustle. You can choose from the area's broad range of hotels and restaurants, from Buitan's upscale Serai, with its highly regarded restaurant situated on the shore, to fun pubs like TJ's in Candidasa, with its Mexican food and margaritas. Some seaside hotels offer a weekly Balinese-food buffet that is a very special (and sometimes spicy) treat for your palate.

The sound of the surf breaking on the shores is part of the oceanside ambience of Candidasa, and the dive sites are part of the seascape. The hulking Gili Tepekong and the four outcrops of Gili Mimpang are right offshore, just a short boat ride by local jukung. A consistent current supports the dense and varied marine life along the shallow reefs and walls that surround these islands. You can depart for snorkel and dive trips from both Candidasa and Padangbai. The two towns are close enough that you can stay in one and make the short trip to the other for a day of diving.

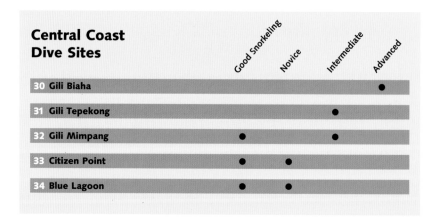

Central Coast Dive Sites	Good Snorkeling	Novice	Intermediate	Advanced
30 Gili Biaha				●
31 Gili Tepekong			●	
32 Gili Mimpang	●		●	
33 Citizen Point	●	●		
34 Blue Lagoon	●	●		

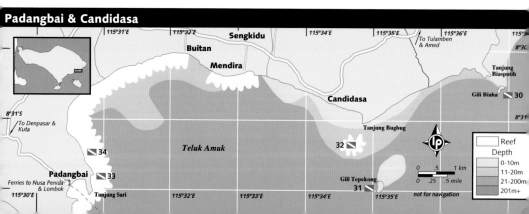

Candidasa's Lost Reefs

The residents of Candidasa learned a tough lesson when nearby barrier-reef corals were harvested to make lime for cement to construct new hotels in the late 1980s. Local hoteliers soon noticed that, to their horror, their beach had washed away and the natural seawall was quickly disappearing. The barrier reef's destruction had resulted in the rapid and continuous erosion of the shoreline.

The coral-reef mining stopped completely in 1991, but the erosion continues. To combat it, international funding was obtained to create a series of rather unsightly T-shaped (and, ironically, cement) barriers. The barriers take some of the force out of the wave action, enabling sand to gather and, hopefully, rebuild the beach. While the barriers have helped somewhat, even they are subject to erosion from the wave action. Candidasa is a testament to the fragility of the coastal environment.

STEFANIE BRENDL/SEA TO SKY

T-shaped barriers have helped control erosion after Candidasa's reef was harvested.

Padangbai is a small, scenic and busy fishing village and port that has only recently begun catering to tourists. The sandy bay, the low-priced bungalows and restaurants, a conveniently located dive center near the local pier and the quick access to some nice dive sites all contribute to the town's relaxing atmosphere.

The reefs around Padangbai have white-sand bottoms and can be stunning when visibility is good. When the channel is calm, you can do a daytrip from Padangbai to the reefs at Nusa Penida. You can also catch the ferry to Lombok, which departs daily from the Padangbai commercial pier.

For a glimpse of one of the region's natural wonders, look for ocean eagles (called *garuda* in Balinese), which nest in the trees of Gili Mimpang's highest island. Up in the hills north of the bay, the walled village of Tenganan is the home of some Bali Aga people, who were the island's original residents before the Hindu migration of the 11th century.

30 | Gili Biaha

Gili Biaha, or Ikuan Island, as the locals call it, is a rocky outcrop just off Tanjung Biasputih (Biasputih Point) a few kilometers northeast of Gili Tepekong. Most divers explore the west side of the island, which is more protected from the surge and offers better diving and boating conditions.

The terrain slopes gradually beyond 37m in the strait between the Bali mainland and the island. Depending on the seas and tides, an incredible current sometimes runs along the slope. Up- and down-currents combine with horizontal jet streams to give divers a real ride. Divers should be comfortable with advanced buoyancy control before attempting to handle these situations and sensations. That said, sometimes it is as calm as a lake here.

Location: East of Tanjung Biasputih

Depth Range: 6.1-40m (20-130ft)

Access: Boat

Expertise Rating: Advanced

The slope offers a great variety of fish life. You will likely see many crinoids filter-feeding from the tops of large barrel sponges bent by the current. The current also brings food particles to the fish in the area. You'll see many species (such as triggerfish and surgeonfish) bobbing up and down catching tidbits as they wash by.

This nutrient-rich current attracts large schools of brilliant-blue yellowtail fusiliers. These fish are as curious as they are abundant. If you stop and wait, chances are that the school will approach almost close enough to touch. This is a great sensation and sometimes ends as quickly as it started, so be alert and prepared to take advantage of the experience.

Coral life isn't thick, but a few large coral heads provide shelter against the current. Divers can duck behind them and look around at the cracks and crevices filled with marine life. Invertebrate life is very plentiful. The coral growth is most dense in the shallow areas, and large sea fans grow along the slope. Species of fans include beautiful gorgonians with snowy-white polyps and blood-red skeletons. Pelagic creatures like dogtooth tuna and sharks also have been seen here.

A diver inspects leather coral.

31 Gili Tepekong

A short boat ride from Buitan or Padangbai, or an even shorter hop from Candidasa, brings divers to Gili Tepekong, a volcanic hump rising out of the water not far from shore.

Location: Southeast of Candidasa

Depth Range: 6.1-40m (20-130ft)

Access: Boat

Expertise Rating: Intermediate

Underwater, this area is covered with medusalike coral heads that vary greatly in size from huge boulders to small sea gardens. They are adorned with blood-red sea fans, tunicates and various sponges. In some spots, the competition for space is incredible—you can't rest on the bottom for fear of damaging the thick coral growth.

Near the island, the bottom is at about 12m and gently slopes away from the island well past 30m.

Gili Tepekong is often done as a drift dive, as strong currents crop up when the tide changes. Your drift dive will take you along the island's wall, which is frequented by a lot of big fish. Golden jacks and huge batfish swim in the open water, while bigeyes and some incredibly colored groupers occupy the cracks and crevices. Blue lobster are found in some holes, and you may see mola-molas near the outer channel facing Nusa Penida, especially during cold upwellings.

Look for big reef creatures, such as grey reef sharks, on the north side of Gili Tepekong. A curious shark may follow divers for the entire dive, probably checking to see if anyone is spearfishing. During the day, you may see whitetip sharks resting in the caves and holes near the boulders along the western edge of the island.

Along the area called **The Canyon** (the shoreward side of the rocky area with the big boulders), strong downcurrents can develop when the tide and surf are active. Do not dive here at these times, as it is very difficult to get out of this strong downward flow and thus is quite dangerous. Be sure your guide is an experienced judge of these conditions.

Currents flush the water and keep it clear, greatly enhancing visibility, which can be 18m or better here. They also bring some very cool water up from the depths. A diver used to tropical water can get downright cold here without a 3m wetsuit.

Candidasa's offshore islands make for great daytrip dive sites.

32 Gili Mimpang

Gili Mimpang consists of the four small islands between Gili Tepekong and the Bali mainland. They are home to ocean eagles, which are revered religious creatures and the namesake of the national airline. The birds nest in trees, and you can see them as they fly over the waves at dawn in search of fish.

Location: Southeast of Candidasa

Depth Range: 6.1-27m (20-90ft)

Access: Boat

Expertise Rating: Intermediate

Underwater, the sea fans along the islands' fringing reef and channels each have at least a dozen crinoids. Some of these brilliant-red sea fans are incredibly colorful, adorned with yellow, black and forest green crinoids.

Magnificent angelfish and clouds of chromis mix with crimson basslets and schools of yellowtails. The large school of bannerfish, commonly found in the deeper water near the outer drop-off, makes for a very colorful photo subject. Napoleon wrasses are seen frequently, as are large grey reef sharks coming in from the deep. You may see eagle rays and large black rays here, as well as lanky leopard sharks. Whitetip sharks like sleeping on the current-swept flats.

This site doesn't get the diver following that it deserves, possibly because of the tricky currents. However, these tricky currents and ocean upwellings are what support the planktonic life that attracts animals like whale sharks, which have been seen in the waters between Gili Mimpang and Gili Tepekong.

Diving is usually done in a circle, going with a current that flows around the rocky islands and back to the boat. The depth here averages only 18m or less, so you can take plenty of time to enjoy the area.

Ocean eagles nest in the high trees of offshore volcanic islands.

33 Citizen Point

It is fun to explore both the shallow and the deep areas of this site, which is punctuated by extremely large old-growth coral bommies hosting crinoids, table corals and lots of fish.

This site's large leather corals resemble sea anemones when they extend their polyps to feed in the current. Look for queen angelfish, oriental sweetlips and copper bigeyes. Scan the sandy seafloor and staghorn thickets for smaller marine life as well, such as groupers, angelfish, feathery lionfish and other colorful tropical fish.

Be ready to encounter larger marine life as you venture from the coral gardens to about 23m, where the sandy flats open up to smaller but equally pristine coral heads. The sightings of grey reef sharks, stingrays and schools of small, silvery tuna and mackerel make it worth the

Location: Northeast of Padangbai

Depth Range: 3-30m (10-100ft)

Access: Boat

Expertise Rating: Novice

swim. Please note that down-currents may occur here, so take care, especially when diving deep. The fish like the currents, so you will find them in abundance when the tide is changing.

Between August and November, colder upwellings bring sightings of wobbegong sharks. These frilly creatures are fun to observe as they swim in a rhythmic, undulating motion. Normally they sit well camouflaged on the bottom, waiting for unsuspecting prey to happen by.

Baitfish school around a diver.

34 Blue Lagoon

Blue Lagoon's shallow reefs are used for introductory dives, night dives and long photo excursions. Staghorn coral patch reefs start in just 3m of water. The reef then opens out onto an area with huge coral bommies, soft leather corals and flowing anemones. The delicate tips of the well-developed plate corals are beautiful, tinged with purple and blue.

Location: North of Padangbai

Depth Range: 1.8-27m (6-90ft)

Access: Boat

Expertise Rating: Novice

The staghorn coral thickets are full of life, with large groupers, schooling sweetlips and clouds of silver chromis. The small damselfish and basslets never seem to stop moving, and butterflyfish are abundant. Clouds of silvery baitfish and sweepers form clusters around many of the corals. Also, you'll see dazzling-white and crimson leaf scorpionfish.

Bali's exceptional invertebrate life can also be seen along this reef. Christmas tree worms of all sizes and colors poke from the rocks and coral heads. Look also for brilliantly colored mantis shrimp and nudibranchs.

Blue Lagoon is known for its large cuttlefish, which can change colors in a heartbeat. Divers can approach quite closely if they keep their movements slow and even, so as not to spook the curious cephalopod. Cuttlefish lay their eggs in the coral thickets, a slow process that you won't regret taking the time to watch.

Divers can access deeper waters by venturing west down the gentle slope and out to the point. More-experienced divers can continue along the wall, which drops vertically to about 24m just off this point. Start deep and work your way back up the wall to the coral gardens to see the best of both underwater worlds.

This shallow, protected site's minute invertebrate life makes it an excellent place for a long and easy night dive. The bottom is reflective, so the site is quite bright when the moon is full, seemingly negating the need for a dive light. There are lots of stonefish in the area, so watch where you place your hands and knees.

Healthy table corals are within snorkeling depths.

Bringing the Reef Back Home

Many people get into underwater photography and videography so they can share the amazing world of the ocean with their friends and family. Unfortunately, the variable lighting conditions and constant motion of a liquid environment make underwater photography a real challenge. Though some embrace it as a new and exciting hobby, others just want to take a few pictures—the simpler the task, the better. Below are a few tips that will help you make the most of your time shooting underwater, whether you are a dedicated or an occasional photographer or videographer.

- Get in the water. No amount of fancy cameras or books on technique can take the place of getting in the water to watch, learn and practice, practice, practice.

- Learn the ways of the wildlife. An underwater photographer is, essentially, a nature photographer. The more you know about a subject's habits, the easier it is to get a good shot.

- Get close…and then get closer. Remember that strobe and video light travels only about 1.5m (5ft) underwater. Learn lighting techniques, as well as animal and fish behavior. With this knowledge, you can closely approach the subjects so they are properly lighted and fill the frame.

- Learn to recognize how colors will appear on film. Color quickly dissipates under the sea. Below 3m (10ft), red tones fade and skin takes on a greenish cast. At 18m (60ft), nearly all color is lost. Artificial light, strobes and color-corrective filters will help reveal the "hidden" colors of your subjects to get those eye-popping shots. For instance, a sponge at 18m (60ft) may appear brown, but when lit by strobes it may be brilliant red on film.

- Make the camera your friend. No matter how cheap or how expensive your setup, once you get to know the strengths and limitations of your equipment, you can exploit them to create nice images. You don't have to spend a fortune on gear to take good photos underwater.

- Develop proper techniques and use buoyancy control. For still photography, remember to frame your subject properly, ensure your lights are properly positioned and hold the camera steady when squeezing the shutter. For videography, don't zoom, and pan only with the action and within scenes. Proper sequencing is the key to telling a fascinating, moving story.

Consumer columns in photo and dive magazines, as well as the knowledgeable staff of many camera shops, can answer your technical questions and help you find suitable equipment. You'll soon be ready to get in the water and have fun!

An artificial light source reveals marine life's true colors.

Sanur Dive Sites

Sanur dive sites are a good option for divers based in southern Bali who want to get wet without traveling far. You'll find upscale hotels, some dark and racy discos and the usual plethora of souvenir shops here. Kites fly high in the onshore breeze during trade-wind season (starting in June). The beach walk that runs the length of the Sanur tourist area is good for strolling and jogging. Afterward, put that weight back on at the variety of pleasant bistros, pubs and hotel dining venues in the area.

Sanur doesn't offer Bali's best diving, but if you want a quick and easy dive or a refresher before exploring Bali's famous sites, it can be worth the trip. Unfortunately, the area is not consistently diveable. Surge and strong currents develop when the moon is full, reducing the visibility and creating less-than-ideal conditions.

A number of beachfront and Sanur-based dive shops will take you diving or snorkeling along the reefs found conveniently near the area's white-sand beaches. These reefs, which offer a variety of corals, are used mostly for training and introductory dives.

Just south of Sanur, dredging around Benoa and an ongoing landfill project at Turtle Island reduce underwater visibility, so diving conditions are poor. The rocky shores of Nusa Dua and Uluwatu farther south are optimal for world-class surfers, but diving here is dangerous most of the year. However, it is a great place to go dolphin-watching, and you may see whales between August and November.

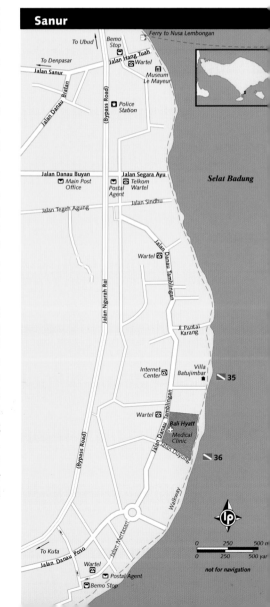

Sanur Dive Sites

	Good Snorkeling	Novice	Intermediate	Advanced
35 Penjor Reef	●	●		
36 Crystal Point	●	●		

35 Penjor Reef

A very pleasant fifteen-minute jukung ride is all it takes to get to this little reef just out from the Villa Batujimbar hotel.

If conditions are good, this can be a very enjoyable dive. It is a perfect site for scuba students and novice divers to practice the basics. The typically mild currents flush the reef and feed the marine life. Be warned: When conditions are bad and currents strong, this site can be somewhat tricky. Make sure your operator knows what he's doing and always bring a safety sausage.

The site slopes very gently down to about 20m, but you don't need to go that deep, as there is plenty to see in the shallows. The reef comes up to about 4m from the surface. This enables the diver to take a long, close look at the vast array of healthy coral.

Look between the big coral heads and bommies to find blue-spotted stingrays. In the distance, a whitetip reef shark will swim by occasionally. You're likely to see colorful reef fish such as butterfly-

Location: East of Villa Batujimbar hotel

Depth Range: 3-20m (10-65ft)

Access: Boat

Expertise Rating: Novice

fish and angelfish, chromis and oriental sweetlips. If you're lucky, you might come across a furry, rust-colored orang-utan crab with brilliant red eyes. They are often found nestled confidently amid the bulbous tentacles of a bubble anemone.

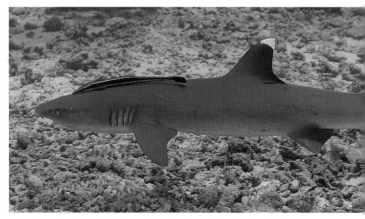

Occasionally, a whitetip reef shark will cruise by Penjor Reef.

36 Crystal Point

Crystal Point is at the tip of a channel that starts opposite the Bali Hyatt Hotel. It's a quick jukung ride along the coast, which is lined with ritzy hotels and white, sandy beaches. This is a good site for training dives. It is also convenient if you haven't been diving for a while and want to do a checkout dive before heading to the major sites upcountry.

Location: Bali Hyatt channel

Depth Range: 3-20m (10-65ft)

Access: Boat

Expertise Rating: Novice

It gradually slopes to a maximum depth of 20m. Coral bommies and table corals dot the rocky bottom. The current-fed reef is quite healthy, with lots of small tropical fish, including the ever-present clouds of golden anthias and chromis damselfish. Look for other critters, like the blue-spotted rays that can be found in the sand under the corals. Whitetip reef sharks sometimes like to cruise this area of the reef. Manta rays also are seen here, but not predictably. This site can be a good snorkeling site, too, when the current is light and visibility is at its best.

The currents can be strong here, especially during a full moon, and it usually gets a little surgy if there's any wave action along the barrier reef. At these times, visibility drops because the white sand stirs up easily.

Colorful anthias and other tropical fish flit around Crystal Point's current-fed reef.

Nusa Penida Dive Sites

The largest of the trio of islands (Penida, Lembongan and Ceningan) off Bali's southeast coast, Nusa Penida sees little in the way of tourism. But the tree-lined beaches and quiet villages sit next to some of the richest reefs in the world.

The eerie coastline of southwestern Penida rises straight up from the sea in rugged foliage-covered cliffs. The island's wild terrain has been the inspiration for many fables and myths. Some Balinese believe that this island is the source of black magic, and that natural disasters like floods and droughts are caused by the giant demon king, Jero Gede Macaling, who comes from Nusa Penida. Because of these beliefs, Balinese are very careful about what they say to the people of Nusa Penida.

Nusa Lembongan is a small but popular daytrip destination just northwest of Nusa Penida. The inhabitants, mostly fisherfolk and farmers, are friendly and down to earth. Mushroom Bay (at the island's southwestern end) was once primarily a surfer's haven, but now attracts a broad spectrum of travelers, including divers. A few dive services have set up shop on the island, so diving here is now both easy to organize and enjoyable.

Sandwiched between Penida and Lembongan is Nusa Ceningan, a tiny, fun-to-explore island. A short bridge spans the narrow channel between Lembongan and Ceningan, making the island easy to access. The village near the bridge is full of fisherfolk and seaweed farmers who work the nearby waters.

Ferries come to Nusa Penida and Lembongan daily from Bali's Padangbai and Benoa harbors. These boats are mainly for people who work in Bali. Several more-upscale ships visit the island daily and offer a plethora of activity packages.

Bali's Gunung Agung looms over the mist-shrouded Nusa Lembongan Island.

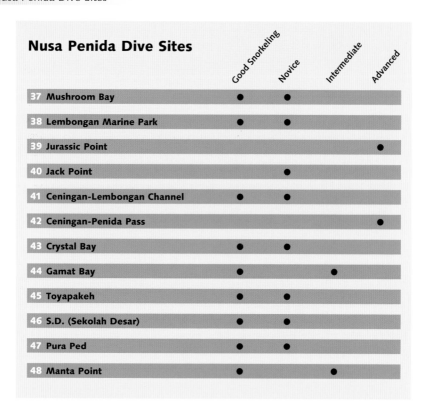

Nusa Penida Dive Sites

	Good Snorkeling	Novice	Intermediate	Advanced
37 Mushroom Bay	●	●		
38 Lembongan Marine Park	●	●		
39 Jurassic Point				●
40 Jack Point		●		
41 Ceningan-Lembongan Channel	●	●		
42 Ceningan-Penida Pass				●
43 Crystal Bay	●	●		
44 Gamat Bay	●		●	
45 Toyapakeh	●	●		
46 S.D. (Sekolah Desar)	●	●		
47 Pura Ped	●	●		
48 Manta Point	●		●	

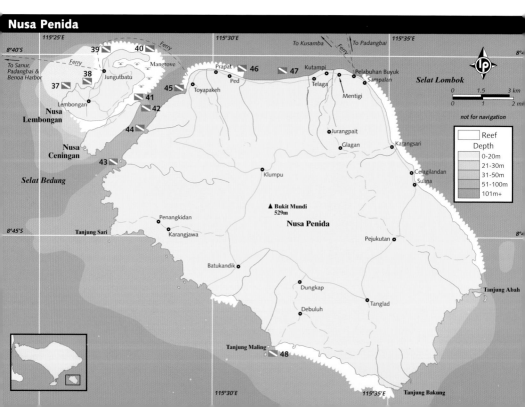

Water Temple

Along the high cliffs of southwestern Nusa Penida, spectacular but precarious bamboo catwalks meander down the 150m sheer cliff face. This death-defying walk leads to water caves that empty fresh water into the sea. Fresh water is scarce on much of Nusa Penida, so people from the clifftop village must make this treacherous trek daily.

Along the pounding surfline, a small Hindu temple stands above a flowing waterfall. The water cascades out of the cliff face, along a rounded rock, and into the sea. Caves have formed on both sides of the rocky outfall. When a boat approaches in the early morning and shuts its engine off, the waterfalls seem to emit a chant-like song. Beautiful and haunting, this music carries across the ocean and dissipates in the horizon.

37 Mushroom Bay

The few upscale hotels along Mushroom Bay's beautiful sandy beaches make this a nice place to stay while visiting Nusa Penida or Lembongan. While the area is busy with boat traffic by day, after 4pm it transforms into a quiet beach where the sun slips tranquilly into the ocean.

The bay isn't great for diving, but is worth snorkeling to take a look at the inlet's thriving corals and invertebrate life. Boat traffic is not a problem, as captains sail slowly and watch for snorkelers.

You'll see many tropical fish, hard corals and sea cucumbers in the usually clear water. Manta rays occasionally feed along the front edge of the bay and don't seem to mind when snorkelers watch them. Keep a respectful distance from

Location: Southwest Nusa Lembongan

Depth Range: 1.5-11m (5-35ft)

Access: Shore or boat

Expertise Rating: Novice

these graceful rays so as not to disturb their feeding habits. Sometimes they won't see a snorkeler approaching head-on when they are filtering plankton with their mouths open wide.

Just outside the bay, a strong offshore current runs out into the channel and off to Bali, so don't go too far without a pick-up boat standing by.

38 Lembongan Marine Park

A dive under the Lembongan Marine Park's pontoon is ideal for beginners and people who are not looking for deep drop-offs or big currents. It is a perfect site for introductory dives or for divers who have been out of the water for a long time. Right under the pontoon is a sandy area where you can adapt to the underwater world and fine-tune your buoyancy control without the risk of damaging delicate corals.

Location: Lembongan Bay

Depth Range: 4.6-12m (15-40ft)

Access: Shore or boat

Expertise Rating: Novice

You can either dive in the park with one of the local dive shops or join a Bali Hai Cruise, which depart daily from Benoa Harbor (southeast Bali) for Nusa Lembongan Bay. People on the cruise can swim, participate in a variety of water-related activities, eat or just relax.

Those who sign up for scuba get an onboard briefing so they know what is in store for them.

Clouds of fish hang out under the mooring hoping to be fed by curious snorkelers. To help you understand what you're looking at, Bali Hai has set up a short reef trail in about 6 to 9m. Beneath the mooring of the activities pontoon, markers inform divers about the different reef attractions. They are easy to find—look for the large concrete blocks set in the sand with handles to hold on to. Artwork and a narrative on the face of each block describe the site. For instance, lionfish are featured at one spot, while flowing sea anemones and their clownfish are the focus of another.

If you venture away from the pontoon in almost any direction you'll find big coral bommies and patch reefs scattered along the sandy bottom. This site is very colorful. Look for cuttlefish as well as octopuses. Pretty clown triggerfish, which have big white dots on their black bellies, are also common at this dive. You may even encounter blue-spotted stingrays around the bommies in the sandy areas.

Currents occasionally pass through here and the bay can get

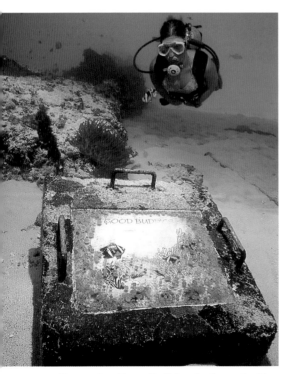

Plaques along the reef trail describe the marine life.

cold, but wetsuits are available through Bali Hai. This is a pleasant dive for those unfamiliar with Indonesian waters or for daytrippers wanting to learn a little more about the sea. Dives to the other reefs in this bay or anywhere around Nusa Penida can also be arranged from here.

Though night diving isn't very common at Lembongan Island, this bay is popular after dark because the bottom is reflective and the corals are home to many invertebrates. Look for hunting lionfish, octopuses and nudibranchs to come out at night here.

39 Jurassic Point

Want to take a fast, fun and wild ride? Just step into the water off western Nusa Lembongan and hang on to your fins, mask and regulator. Make sure you go with an experienced dive guide, listen carefully to the dive briefing and dive only in the right conditions. As one famed guide put it, "This may be the best dive of your life, the worst dive of your life or the last dive of your life." Currents here can be very strong, but the wild, roiling action can make the dive worth your while if you're an adrenaline junkie.

Location: West-central Nusa Lembongan

Depth Range: 7.6-40m+ (25-130ft+)

Access: Boat

Expertise Rating: Advanced

Strong tidal and interisland currents from about 18m down make the waters unpredictable. One hour they can be

The swift currents of the reef slopes can be unpredictable, but they bring out the fish life.

calm and unmoving, and the next a 4-knot blast can grab you and take you on the ride of a lifetime. Down- and up-currents and upwellings from deep below all add to the excitement of this amazing full-speed roller-coaster ride. Add occasional temperature changes, which can cool the tropical water as much as 10°C, and this dive has a chilling effect unmatched anywhere in the world.

The sloping reeftop flats start at about 12m. They are extremely colorful, with lots of life teeming amid the coral bommies, sponges and sea fans. These flats lead to a ledgy area called Jurassic Point. It was once known as Blue Corner, but since it really isn't that blue, the name has been changed.

In this wild environment, rays are often seen hovering in midwater. Flying full force into a school of large black stingrays can be a real eye-opener! These rays usually lie buried in the sand, but they like to hover above when the current cooks, presumably catching food as the water whisks it by. On calm days, you can approach them as they lie in the sand, but be careful not to disturb or threaten them, as a flick of a tail can inflict a nasty wound.

Look out into the blue for the big boys. Jurassic Point is an interesting site where you'll see sharks on occasion, as well as other denizens of the deep. By far the most fascinating of these is the mola-mola, or ocean sunfish. This fish looks unlike anything else. Its tiny mouth, huge dorsal fins, small tail and set-back eyes make the ocean sunfish seem like a biological mistake. Sunfish can be seen here during what is thought to be their mating season, which runs from June to October.

Sunfish

The oceanic sunfish, or mola-mola, is usually a pelagic creature. These animals are rarely seen near coral reefs, preferring to drift with the ocean currents in pursuit of their favorite food (purple jellyfish) and feed on plankton. The creature's body length can exceed 2.5m and its height can be double the length. Its fins and stubby tail are made of rough skin similar to a shark's. Oceanic sunfish have been seen floating at the surface with birds pecking parasites from their cartilaginous sides.

Mola-molas come near the reef only briefly, presumably to mate and preen. At this time, clouds of bannerfish and even French angelfish arrive to clean the parasites from their bizarre bodies.

In Bali, mola-molas may be seen at any time of year around the reefs of Nusa Lembongan, Gili Tepekong, Tulamben Drop-off, Amed Wall and the *Liberty* wreck. They are seen most often at Lembongan's Jurassic Point, where they come to mate in the wild, cold waters. Prime time to see them is from late July to early September.

TONY MEDCRAFT

40 Jack Point

This reef is a great place for snorkeling, easy shallow dives and magnificent current rides for more-experienced divers. Dives start at the northeast tip of Lembongan, near the mangroves along the coast. Look for staghorn corals and seaweed farms in the shallows. The currents tend to be calm down to 11 or 12m. More-experienced divers can catch the flow and coast over big barrel sponges, sea fans and lots of fish. Notice the odd, pretzel-like shapes of the sponges and corals—a result of the currents.

At 21 to 24m, schools of sweetlips flash their bright yellow bodies in symmetrical formation. You'll see the most fish action near the tip and along the wall below 24m. Keep an eye on the blue, where dogtooth tuna and whitetip sharks occasionally appear.

Location: Northeast Nusa Lembongan

Depth Range: 4.6-27m (15-90ft)

Access: Boat

Expertise Rating: Novice

The reef's huge angelfish inhabitants make this site a fish photographer's paradise. Colorful juvenile regal angelfish, stealthy yellowmask angelfish, striking blue-ringed angelfish and some very big emperor angelfish all hang out near the coral bommies.

You may notice coral damage to the south. Villagers removed the coral to make plots for their seaweed farms, but it is slowly recovering in some places.

41 Ceningan-Lembongan Channel

This passage between Nusa Ceningan and Nusa Lembongan is a shallow drift snorkel. The adventure usually begins near the maze of seaweed farms at the southwest end of the channel, then heads northeast with the mild current. Some snorkelers use a kayak to paddle the mangroves, then jump in where it looks interesting.

This drift snorkel can provide some fun surprises. The channel is lined with mangroves that house sea stars, mudskippers and lots of small juvenile fish. These creatures use the mangroves for protection as they grow and flourish. Large fish often venture into this channel at high tide to forage for food. Large jacks are occasionally seen from the suspension bridge that runs between the islands.

Location: East of Nusa Lembongan

Depth Range: 0.6-4.6m (2-15ft)

Access: Boat

Expertise Rating: Novice

42 Ceningan-Penida Pass

The southeast side of Nusa Ceningan offers a hair-raising ride in what is said to be one of the world's deepest natural channels. It separates Nusa Ceningan from Nusa Penida and is suitable only for experienced divers.

The dive, which starts at the northern end of Nusa Ceningan, isn't for the faint of heart. Reef corals at the start of the dive lead up to a wall where the brisk current sweeps you toward the open sea. Strong currents running along the sheer wall opposite Gamat and Crystal Bays provide high-voltage action and a chance to see big dogtooth tuna, groupers, bull jacks and sharks. The wall is adorned with soft corals, tubastrea corals and sea fans.

Location: West of Nusa Penida

Depth Range: 6.1-40m+ (20-130ft+)

Access: Boat

Expertise Rating: Advanced

Down- and up-currents make this dive tricky, so it should be undertaken only by experienced divers looking for swift drifts and big sea life. Be sure to have a fast boat ready to pick you up before you get to the mouth of the channel. The whirlpools and converging currents at the mouth are dangerous, so divers should exit before getting to this frothy area.

Soft corals filter-feed in the brisk current that flows through the Ceningan-Penida Pass.

43 Crystal Bay

Much of this dive site is protected and relatively shallow, offering enjoyable conditions for divers of all levels. The bay has two entrances, and a large rock sits in its center. Be careful when diving along the outside edge of this central rock, as the current can be strong and can sweep divers into very tricky conditions. An experienced guide can help prevent a disoriented diver from taking a wrong turn and getting swept away.

When near the drop-off, look for large creatures like eagle rays, dogtooth tuna, sharks and an occasional bumphead wrasse. Schooling surgeonfish are abundant in some spots.

Inner Crystal Bay is tame. Its splendid large coral formations are havens for marine life. Large schools of glassy sweepers form living walls under many of the overhangs. Look at these undercuts for bottom-oriented basslets, which can often be seen swimming upside down along the coral. Also, keep an eye out for the brilliant-orange soft corals that grow here. Look for extremely large angelfish and a monster-sized eel while exploring the area.

A few surprises await observant divers at the sand patch, found close to the lone giant tridacna clamshell (poached long ago). Big balls of striped catfish are one such treat. In one area along the rocky northern shore, a

Location: West Nusa Penida

Depth Range: 3-37m (10-120ft)

Access: Boat

Expertise Rating: Novice

big hole forms a small cave that divers can carefully swim into. Resting sharks sometimes inhabit it.

Large numbers of soft leather corals thrive in the cool water temperatures typical of the bay. In one area, the large coral ears are packed together, carpeting a broad expanse of the seafloor.

Big balls of striped catfish cruise the sand patches of Crystal Bay.

44 Gamat Bay

In the right conditions, Gamat Bay is a beautiful dive and a great snorkeling site, too. An incredible variety and quantity of aquarium fish—such as golden and violet anthias, chromis and damselfish—dart about huge bommies in the shallower reaches of the inner bay and along the steep slope at the bay's mouth.

Location: West Nusa Penida

Depth Range: 3-27m (10-90ft)

Access: Boat

Expertise Rating: Intermediate

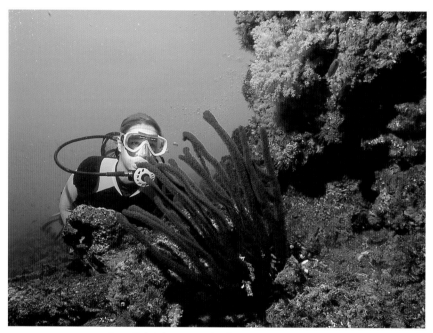

Beautiful violet octocorals adorn Gamat Bay's wall.

The bay is no more than 12m deep, and the bommies come up to within 2m of the surface. Squid like to swim near the surface and will approach you quite closely. If they feel threatened, they may flash brilliant colors and zip off as quickly as they appeared.

The reef transitions into a fairly steep slope, almost a wall, on the outside edge of the bay. Look for cuttlefish and moray eels under the coral heads here. Keep glancing out into the blue from time to time as, with a bit of luck, you may see eagle rays and reef sharks out there.

The reef drops below 40m, so don't forget to monitor your depth as you look at everything this site has to offer. It is wise to stay above 30m, as the currents can be very strong. Make sure that your operator is familiar with local conditions and knows how to read the water and tides.

45 Toyapakeh

You'll find this site just off the Toyapakeh pier at a recreation area used by a few daytrip companies. It is at the northwest end of the narrow, current-swept and extremely deep Ceningan Pass.

The constant current makes this a great spot for fish life. Ideally, the current runs along the slope and out toward the Selat Lombok instead of into the pass. This allows you to dip down early in the dive to 24m or so. Here you can see the fish congregating around the large coral heads and along the hard-coral shelves that make up the bottom.

From there, you can drift over fields of hard corals embedded with coral-covered tridacna clams. Lots of small tropicals, glassy sweepers, basslets and anthias thrive in this current-swept environment.

Location: Northwest Nusa Penida

Depth Range: 3-37m (10-120ft)

Access: Boat

Expertise Rating: Novice

Divers should start to ascend before getting too close to the end of the pass, where the current tends to pick up again and create tiny whirlpools between the islands. Finish in the calm shallows looking for the eels and other marine life that enjoy the hard corals of Toyapakeh.

Snorkelers should stay closer to shore (away from the currents) to experience the flourishing coral gardens.

46 | S.D. (Sekolah Desar)

The reefs surrounding Nusa Penida have seen relatively few divers over the years. This is one reason that the coral gardens are world-class and the profusion of life is incredible. There are few reefs in the world that can match this dive site, known simply as S.D. because of the public school *(sekolah desar)* found on shore.

Diving here is normally a drift of some sort. When the current is running it can be a fast ride, but at slack tide the current can wind down to nonexistent. To duck out of the current, divers can hover in the sandy lee behind the big coral structures. From there, it is easy to watch the marine life. Look for smaller fish and nudibranchs in the protected areas of the bommies. Huge queen angel-

Location: North-central Nusa Penida

Depth Range: 3-40m (10-130ft)

Access: Boat

Expertise Rating: Novice

fish and big pufferfish are the norm here as well. Mola-molas, whitetip reef sharks, mantas and even an orca have all been seen along this reef.

Crinoids fight for space on the big sponges that grow everywhere. Platter corals grow high and wide. Groups of anemones feed on the nutrients brought in by the currents. Look for percula clownfish on the anemones. These bright orange and energetic little guys inspire amusement and awe, as they battle the awesome currents to stake their place in the anemone's tentacles.

You might see a sea snake at S.D. While they are beautiful to watch as they wind through the corals, it is easy to forget that they are highly poisonous. Their mellow personality means that divers are rarely at risk of being bitten, but be sure not to bother them.

A pontoon was set up along this reef to create a mooring for the Quicksilver tour company. The gross placement of heavy cement footings destroyed the old-growth corals that flourished here for many hundreds of years. It is a sad testament to the fragility of coral reefs and how easily they can be destroyed.

Anemones withdraw their tentacles at dusk.

47 Pura Ped

This reef along Nusa Penida's north coast slopes down to about 50m, but you don't have to go very deep to see some magnificent stuff.

Pura Ped makes a superb drift dive. Currents can be strong, so enjoy the ride but don't forget to bring your safety sausage. These currents have produced some fascinating coral formations that resemble modern sculptures. Hard corals twist and stretch into medusalike shapes. The rich coral cover is home to many tropical fish.

Occasionally, a manta ray or a school of barracuda will sweep in from the blue along the gradual slope that empties into the deep straits. Whitetip reef sharks sleep under table corals by day and forage for food at night. Green moray eels peek their heads out from the crevices, and groupers and sweetlips are common along the shelves. Divers have even encountered a half-dozen sea snakes on a single dive.

In the deeper waters, the nutrient-rich sea quickly absorbs the light. The terrain is a little more current-swept, and wire

Location: North-central Nusa Penida

Depth Range: 3-37m (10-120ft)

Access: Boat

Expertise Rating: Novice

corals sprout like giant corkscrews from the reef. It is here that an encounter with a giant bat ray, which can grow to nearly 2m in diameter, is most likely to occur. The highlight of your dive may be seeing a group of these rays or a 3m long great hammerhead shark gracefully swimming along at a depth of 20m.

On the smaller end of the scale, there are emperor angelfish, some friendly titan triggerfish, bannerfish and (if you can spot one) well-camouflaged scorpionfish. Brilliant angelfish hide under the coral heads that dot the reef.

The colorful reeftop makes for a pleasant safety stop or snorkel excursion. The corals are in great condition, attracting

Pura Ped's shallow reeftop makes for a colorful safety stop or snorkel excursion.

swarms of anthias and basslets. Blue-spotted stingrays hide in the sand under the coral heads, while reef octopuses search for food.

This site has the potential for an interesting night dive, though few people actually visit here after dark. Those who do should check the shallows for nudibranchs, shrimp, crabs and a few other surprises. The beauty of the Milky Way on the boat ride back to shore makes the entire excursion worthwhile.

48 Manta Point

Manta Point is best dived from local Nusa Lembongan boats. In calm conditions, any capable diver can enjoy Manta Point. Even snorkelers will enjoy watching giant devilfish gracefully coast below them. Weather, surf, wind, current and tide can make this site dangerous. So, if your guide says this dive can't be done, don't argue!

Manta Point and its smaller neighboring rock, Bat Rock, sit along the wild cliffline of southern Nusa Penida. The rocks are home to fruit bats (flying mammals that resemble small foxes), which roost on the islands by day and fly to the mainland at night to forage for fruit and other edibles. Their dusk passage looks like Mother Nature's version of a Dracula movie.

Location: South Nusa Penida

Depth Range: 3-24m (10-80ft)

Access: Boat

Expertise Rating: Intermediate

During certain times of the year, especially in April, May and June, mantas gather along this reef. Here they visit cleaning stations, mate and give birth to their young. They also feed by swimming into the current with their immense mouths wide open. The mantas come in along an invisible path, usually moving against the current, and hover over a series of cleaning stations. Look for the small cleaner wrasses and butterflyfish that service the mantas.

At times, the mantas literally line up in a long parade around the outer edges of the rocks. You may even see them break the surface and slap the water with their wings. Mantas come in all sizes and colors, from almost light gray with brilliant white underbellies, to jet black with just a speck of white on their mandibles.

For an up-close experience, patiently wait nearby and breathe as lightly as possible. Don't chase or try to ride them. The curious ones will come by for a look, allowing you to get an up-close view of their power and grace.

Fruit bats fly above Bat Rock.

Lombok Dive Sites

Lombok's Gili Islands offer visitors calm and crystal-clear waters, white-sand beaches, swaying coconut palms and lots of diving. Dive sites here are accessible year-round, with generally calm waters and short boat rides to most sites. The sloping coral-covered reefs that surround the three islands are good for all levels of scuba enthusiasts. Drift dives are the norm, and some fascinating critter dives and challenging deep dives can be found in select spots for more-experienced divers. Local dive shops offer many specialty courses in this varied marine environment. The Gilis are a marine reserve, so the collecting of marine life, corals and shells is not allowed.

The Gilis feature a range of enjoyable vacation environments. Because no cars or motorbikes are allowed out here, it is easy to find a quiet, secluded home away from home. However, those who want a little more action while on vacation can find that here as well.

Gili Trawangan is the largest of the three islands, and has the biggest reputation as a "party" isle. It also receives the most visitors, the majority of which find lodging and services along the hotel and dive-shop strip. Accommodations and

Gili Trawangan's lookout point offers the best view of the low-lying Gili Islands.

restaurants are varied, so something can be found to suit most tastes. Trawangan also has the highest elevation, and the short hike up the hill offers a great view of the islands. It is also a good place to watch the sunset.

The tourist-friendly island of Gili Meno has the smallest population and is perhaps the quietest of these little islands. You can circumnavigate it on foot in about 90 minutes, and it's not hard to find a secluded little beach of your own here.

Gili Air is still quite primitive, dotted with coconut groves and *kampung* (villages). Visitors can choose among accommodations scattered around the island. Most are simple bungalows with a sea view and fan. Breakfast is normally included in the price of the room. The many good restaurants serve varied dishes, from local to Western cuisine.

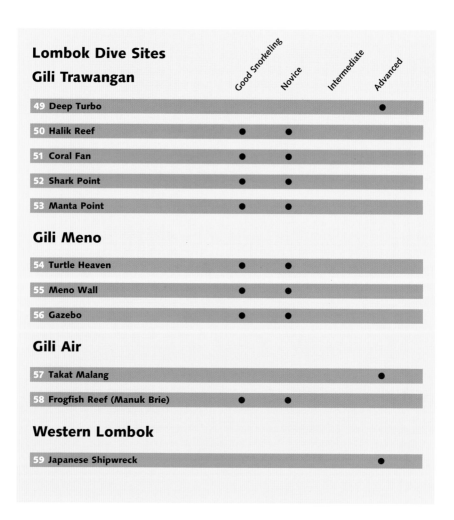

Lombok Dive Sites
Gili Trawangan

	Good Snorkeling	Novice	Intermediate	Advanced
49 Deep Turbo				●
50 Halik Reef	●	●		
51 Coral Fan	●	●		
52 Shark Point	●	●		
53 Manta Point	●	●		

Gili Meno

54 Turtle Heaven	●	●		
55 Meno Wall	●	●		
56 Gazebo	●	●		

Gili Air

57 Takat Malang				●
58 Frogfish Reef (Manuk Brie)	●	●		

Western Lombok

59 Japanese Shipwreck				●

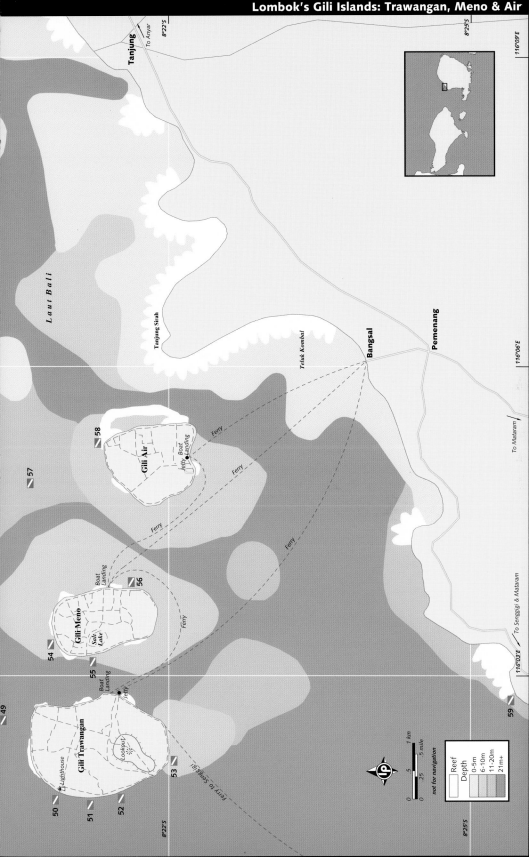

Tanjung

To Anyar

8°22'S

8°25'S

116°09'E

Laut Bali

Tanjung Sirah

Teluk Kombal

Bangsal

Pemenang

116°06'E

To Mataram

57

58

Gili Air

Boat Landing

Jetty

Ferry

Ferry

Ferry

Ferry

Ferry

54

Gili Meno

Salt Lake

Boat Landing

55

56

49

Boat Landing

Jetty

Gili Trawangan

Lighthouse

Lookout

50

51

52

53

Ferry to Senggigi

8°22'S

8°25'S

116°03'E

To Senggigi & Mataram

59

1 km

.5

.5 mile

.25

0

0

not for navigation

Reef

Depth

0-5m

6-10m

11-20m

21m+

Gili Air Turtle Hatchery

Less than 1% of the turtles born in the wild survive until sexual maturity (about 20 years old). Unfortunately, their chances of survival are worsening as human impact increases. The tourist development of many of the turtle's natural nesting areas has decreased the space that they have to lay their eggs. Indonesians collect the eggs to sell as food items

at the local markets, and turtles are hunted for their meat (considered a delicacy in Bali) and shells. Consequently, many species of marine turtles throughout Indonesia and the world are now endangered.

The folks at Reefseekers on Gili Air are active conservationists and have worked with turtles since 1994. They send scouts into the local markets to rescue the eggs, which are transplanted to artificial nests at the nursery. Incubation takes about 60 days. The turtles are raised to a stage where they can fend for themselves.

When Reefseekers started this program, there were virtually no turtles seen in the wild around the Gilis. As a testament to the program's success, sea turtles are now seen on almost every local dive.

Hawksbill turtles grace many Gili dive sites.

49 Deep Turbo

This series of deep reefs and channels is a 15-minute boat ride (on a calm day) north of Gili Trawangan. Each of these wonderfully decorated reefs is covered in large tube sponges, rope sponges and big barrel sponges. Lacy coral flourishes in the undercuts and sea fans dot the reef.

Small fish cover the coral outcrops. Garden eels congregate in the white, sandy valleys, and you may see whitetip sharks asleep here. Look for leopard sharks resting in the sand near the overhangs. Whitetip and blacktip reef sharks can also been seen swimming freely, but don't approach them too closely or they

Location: North Gili Trawangan

Depth Range: 18-40m (60-130ft)

Access: Boat

Expertise Rating: Advanced

will swim away. Be patient and they will come closer as they become more comfortable with your presence.

Small groups of batfish sometimes break away from the site's huge shoal to circle around divers. You may find juvenile batfish hiding in the cover of

gorgonians. Also, look for bluestripe snapper, blueface angelfish, lyretail blue triggerfish and other fish.

The marine life at this dive varies depending on how the current runs. On days when it is rushing, divers may see schools of as many as 70 bumphead parrotfish, thick schools of jacks and other pelagic fish. The best time to see fish action here is during the tide change, but currents can be tricky, so stick close to your guide.

Juvenile batfish seeks shelter within the lush coral.

50 Halik Reef

Divers of all expertise levels can enjoy this drift over chromis-filled Halik Reef. The assorted bommies and low-growing coral gardens lead you to a slope where coral formations offer cracks and overhangs filled with soldierfish and copper sweepers.

Location: West Gili Trawangan

Depth Range: 3.7-18m (12-60ft)

Access: Boat

Expertise Rating: Novice

Mantas are seen here from March to May, though February and June also offer a good chance to see them. Divers may also see a plethora of green and hawksbill turtles eating hydroids.

Undulating tropical fish, soft corals and sea fans dot the current-fed side of the outcrops and add a lot of color to the site. Look closely for the large, camouflaged stonefish nestled in the feeding, outstretched tubastrea polyps. Also, keep an eye out for small critters, including nudibranchs and *Tridacna squamosa* clams. You may catch a glimpse of whitetip reef sharks and giant trevallies along the deepest parts of the dive.

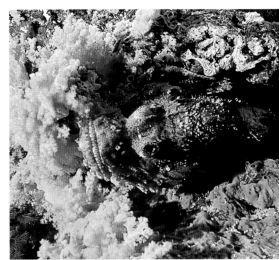

Watch out for stonefish lurking amid the soft corals.

51 Coral Fan

This site is aptly named for its abundance of large, white-polyped gorgonian fans with bright-red skeletons. These grow on the big coral bommies of this site's shallow reeftop.

You'll find other types of hard corals interspersed along the bottom at 3 to 5m, surrounded by lots of reef fish and tropicals. Small copper sweepers especially like to congregate here. The shallow corals and colorful fish life make Coral Fan a good choice for snorkeling in the Gilis.

Divers often see titan triggerfish and clown triggerfish on this site's outside wall, which drops from 8 to 30m. The

Location: West Gili Trawangan

Depth Range: 4.6-26m (15-85ft)

Access: Boat

Expertise Rating: Novice

strong currents that feed the wall's healthy corals and fans make drift diving the order of the day. The slopes have varied fish life, including a good selection of scorpionfish, so be careful where you put your hands.

Outcrops are just dripping with coral at Coral Fan.

52 | Shark Point

This is one of the Gilis' most popular dives. It is normally done as a drift dive heading toward the point at the center of Gili Trawangan's western coast. It can be dived at three levels—there are places for deep dives, midwater drifts and shallow coral-garden exploration.

Location: West Trawangan

Depth Range: 3-37m (10-120ft)

Access: Boat

Expertise Rating: Novice

The coral growth here is thick, with sea fans along the wall and some very large formations along the deeper reaches near the channel. Look for the healthy soft-coral trees fed by the strong currents. The best place to see gorgonian fans and sea whips is along this current-fed outer hill.

Bannerfish and Moorish idols decorate the reef with their high-contrast black-and-yellow bodies. You'll see them moving around the coral formations. Look for mantas at the current-swept point, as well as reef sharks and occasional rays. Divers have also seen mobula rays. A mobula's head is similar to a manta's, but its mandibles are closer together.

Most divers end this dive along the upper reef flats before the tip of the point. Carry a safety sausage, as the currents can sweep

divers off the point into the open sea. Cuttlefish, blue-spotted stingrays, turtles, chromis, basslets and other colorful reef fish thrive in this area's shallow water.

Striped snapper school over the shallow coral.

53 | Manta Point

Aptly named Manta Point is generally an easy dive that makes for a fine drift when the current is running. The peak season for mantas is from March to May, though February and June also offer good possibilities to see them, and mantas can be seen sporadically year-round. As many as 17 mantas have been seen here at one time.

Location: South Gili Trawangan

Depth Range: 6.1-27m (20-90ft)

Access: Boat

Expertise Rating: Novice

Though the visibility at this site can be quite good, local guide Adi Sucipto claims that the nutrients carried into the water by runoff make the mantas more active. So, the lower visibility that divers may encounter during the rainy months of November and December can actually be a blessing in disguise.

Even if you don't see mantas, this is a rewarding site for divers of all abilities. You'll find lobster and moray eels in the rocky parts of the reef. Look also

for cuttlefish hovering over the corals, flashing their brilliant colors. The cuttlefish's ability to camouflage itself is unsurpassed—it is even able to mimic the reddish algae found along the bottom here.

Locals joke that Manta Point is the spot where "old" turtles gather. The turtles found here are larger than the ones seen on the east side of the island, and their shells are covered with barnacles and algae.

Manta fly-bys are common year-round.

54 Turtle Heaven

Turtle Heaven certainly lives up to its name, with lots of green and hawksbill turtles feeding on sponges and hydroids amid the reeftop coral gardens. Divers are just about guaranteed to see a turtle here. In fact, divers may see a half-dozen turtles on a single dive.

You can usually approach the turtles quite closely, making it easy to take great photos. Resist the temptation to touch them—it disturbs their eating, affects their breathing and will make them more wary of other divers.

Divers can go over the wall and down a sharp slope that drops to 24m. Here you'll have a pretty good chance of seeing whitetip sharks, tridacna clams and

Location: North Gili Meno

Depth Range: 3-24m (10-80ft)

Access: Boat

Expertise Rating: Novice

garden eels out in the sand flats. Titan triggerfish are also seen here. Sea snakes like to course the wall and look through the rubble for prey. They eat small crabs, shrimp, fish and shellfish. Scorpionfish also like this habitat, and clownfish and their anemone hosts are abundant along the reef edge.

Turtle Heaven lives up to its name.

Look for chromis, basslets and other colorful reef fish in the shallow waters. The shallow corals are starting to regrow after being damaged by El Niño a while back.

The current here is usually mild, but it sometimes gets strong at low tide. Plan on a drift dive when the water is moving. Carrying a safety sausage is always a good idea.

55 Meno Wall

A drift drive along Meno Wall is usually quite a ride. Divers drop into the channel between Trawangan and Meno and descend to the wall that drops from 6 to 27m.

Look for whitetip sharks sleeping in the sand in the channel. The wall's north end is an excellent place to see green and hawksbill sea turtles. You'll also find a variety of fish, plus an abundant assortment of invertebrates and nudibranchs. Lionfish, chromis and spotted rays are also part of the standard fare. The coral here is not in good

Location: West Gili Meno

Depth Range: 4.6-27m (15-90ft)

Access: Boat

Expertise Rating: Novice

shape due to El Niño, but soft corals adorn some of the reeftop along the wall's upper reaches.

At night, a quick 15-minute ride in the fast current that sweeps along the wall can

A diver follows a banded sea snake over Meno Wall's hard-coral garden.

be a real thrill. The drift ends in a shallow eddy where divers can use their remaining air in calm water. Here you'll see all kinds of nocturnal activities. Sleeping fish rest in the corals and rocky holes. Macrophotographers can get shots of a variety of nudibranchs, including Spanish dancers, as well as lobster and crabs.

56 Gazebo

This site in front of the Gili Meno harbor is an attractive shallow dive, just 5 to 18m deep. Snorkelers also like this site because the water is generally clear and the sandy bottom makes it easy to see marine life.

Divers will find a variety of fish, including Moorish idols, angelfish and parrotfish. Smaller tropicals and the unusual mantis shrimp may also pop up.

Turtles are common here, as in most of the Gilis' shallow reefs. Scorpionfish can be found blending into the bottom

Location: Southeast Gili Meno

Depth Range: 5-18m (17-60ft)

Access: Boat

Expertise Rating: Novice

and moray eels peek out from the reef's holes and crevices.

57 | Takat Malang

This is one of the area's premier dive sites and can be a real treat when conditions are calm, as visibility is often 30m or better at high tide, especially if it hasn't rained. The blue water and brilliant white-sand bottom provide a stunning backdrop for this natural seascape. A sloping wall leads to a series of deep reefs on loaf-shaped reef bases at 3 to 40m.

Location: Open water north of Gili Air

Depth Range: 14-40m (45-130ft)

Access: Boat

Expertise Rating: Advanced

There are about ten of these big, loaf-shaped reefs within a very large area, so you would need to do a series of dives over a couple of days to even try to see everything. The deep canyon of the most northerly site has multiple fans and lots of fish. It is especially worth seeing if there is a brisk current, because the fish life is most profuse.

Take your time and go slowly from one reef to the next. The overhangs and mini-walls throughout the area have large sponges, an excellent array of large fan corals, sea whips and soft corals.

Sea whips sprout from Takat Malang's mini-walls.

Fish life is also excellent, making it worth doing several dives just to see the diversity of species and habitats. Look for whitetip sharks, big schools of batfish, groupers and large schools of sweetlips.

This is a multilevel dive that starts deep and ends somewhat shallow if currents and time permit. Though strong currents mean more fish life, this is also a very good dive at slack tide—you'll spend less air and energy trying to stay in one place, allowing you to stay down longer and see more. Open water decompression may be necessary here.

58 Frogfish Reef (Manuk Brie)

Frogfish Reef, also known as Manuk Brie, is a favorite site among naturalists and macrophotographers. The dive can be done along the site's wall, but the real surprises for divers and snorkelers are along the upper reaches. The upper reef terrain consists of a coral garden with a vast abundance of the smaller reef fish in an assortment of colors and shapes.

Location: North Gili Air

Depth Range: 4.6-20m (15-65ft)

Access: Boat

Expertise Rating: Novice

You'll find a plethora of odd critters, such as leaf fish, stonefish, scorpionfish, many nudibranchs, morays, rare species of lionfish, flying gurnards, cleaner shrimp, leaf ghost pipefish and mantas. At night, divers will see lots of crabs, shrimp and lobster.

Also, look here for the site's namesake, the unusual frogfish. Frogfish, or anglerfish, are very difficult to find—they look like pieces of sponge or coral. A frogfish catches prey by extending a spine over its head. The spine has a small piece of skin on the end that looks like a worm. When a fish swims by and tries to eat the lure—gulp!—it's swallowed whole by the frogfish, whose mouth extends forward to suck in its prey. Frogfish can eat fish as large as they are.

Keep your eyes open to see the odd ghost pipefish and the beautiful and not-easily-seen ornate ghost pipefish, which are in the same family as seahorses. Pipefish are seen only during the rainy season. The lacy appendages of these beautiful, well-camouflaged creatures make them a stunning subject to behold and capture on film.

59 Japanese Wreck

This deep technical dive is well worth the effort for properly trained divers. During WWII, a fisherman saw this Japanese ship go down near his small fishing village along the Lombok coast. The wreck's exact whereabouts have been known for more than a decade, but it has been visited infrequently because of its extreme

Location: Northwestern Lombok

Depth Range: 41-47m (135-155ft)

Access: Boat

Expertise Rating: Advanced

depth. This ship was rediscovered by Simon Liddiard of Blue Marlin Dive Centre on Gili Trawangan, the only technical-diving facility in Lombok.

This small but extremely picturesque WWII Japanese vessel is still laden with sake bottles and other artifacts, which divers should leave intact. The ship sits upright along the 47m sandy bottom and rises to 41m. Visibility is usually good here. Though moderate to strong currents between 6 and 18m are possible, they are not likely to affect the wreck itself.

The ship is adorned with tubastrea corals and soft corals. The fish life is impressive, with schools of batfish hovering over the bow and at midships at the tiny bridge. You'll see legions of lionfish aft, midships and astern on the top deck. Scorpionfish rest hidden in many places. The wreck's intact stern and rudder have depth charges, which resemble small barrels, littering the seafloor around them. Pene-

tration is not advised, as quarters are tight and you could damage the coral growth.

Dive operators rarely anchor at this site, so tech divers do open-water, free-floating decompressions. The plankton carried by the upper currents is interesting, and helps pass the time during the lengthy stops.

Keep an eye on this area in the future, as a number of other possible shipwreck sites have been identified and are in the process of being explored.

A diver approaches the shipwreck's rudder.

Deep Diving

Opportunities to dive deep abound in Bali and Lombok. Many attractions are beyond 40m (130ft), the recognized maximum depth limit of sport diving. Before venturing beyond these limits, it is imperative that divers be specially trained in deep diving and/or technical diving.

Classes will teach you to recognize symptoms of nitrogen narcosis and proper decompression procedures when doing deep or repetitive deep dives. Remember, emergency facilities in Bali and Lombok are limited. Know your limits and don't push your luck when it comes to depth.

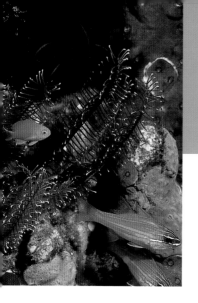

Marine Life

The habitats and conditions of the marine environment around Bali and Lombok support one of the most biologically diverse and abundant coral reef systems on the planet. Invertebrate life is especially noteworthy. Many species, though similar to those seen elsewhere, are believed to be endemic to Bali. Also, many fish are undescribed and may be new species or subspecies. The variety of species attracts marine scientists, underwater photographers, amateur biologists and, of course, divers from around the world. Diving in Bali and Lombok is somewhat in its infancy, making this a real frontier for discovery.

Common names are used freely but are notoriously inaccurate and inconsistent. The two-part scientific name, usually shown in italics, is more precise. It consists of a genus name followed by a species name. A genus is a group of closely related species that share common features. A species is a recognizable group within a genus whose members are capable of interbreeding. Where the species or genus is unknown, the naming reverts to the next known level: family (F), order (O), class (C) or phylum (Ph).

Common Vertebrates

spinecheek anemonefish
Premnas biaculeatus

clownfish
Amphiprion ocellaris

Clark's anemonefish
Amphiprion clarkii

pink anemonefish
Amphiprion perideraion

maiden goby
Valenciennea puellaris

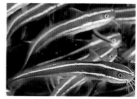

striped catfish
Plotosus lineatus

rabbitfish
Siganus sp.

lunar-tailed big-eye
Priacanthus tayenus

yellow-ribbon sweetlips
Plectorhinchus polytaenia

humpback snapper
Lutjanus gibbus

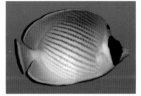

coral cod
Cephalopholis miniata

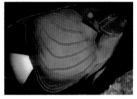

bignose unicornfish
Naso vlamingii

shaded batfish
Platax pinnatus

masked butterflyfish
Chaetodon adiergastos

bluering angelfish
Pomacanthus annularis

variegated lizardfish
Synodus variegatus

ring-tailed cardinalfish
Apogon aureus

ribbon eel
Rhinomuraena quaesita

manta ray
Manta birostris

spotted wobbegong
Orectolobus maculatus

ocean sunfish
Mola mola

Common Invertebrates

emperor shrimp
Periclimenes imperator

hingebeak shrimp
Rhynchocinetes durbanensis

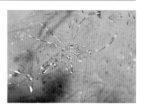

sponge cleaner shrimp
Leandrites cyrtorhyncus

mantis shrimp
Odontodactylus scyllarus

coral crab
F. *Grapsidae*

hermit crab
F. *Diogenidae*

gorgonian fan coral
F. *Gorgonidae*

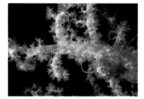

soft coral tree
Dendronephthya sp.

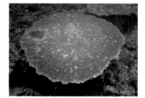

table coral
F. *Acropridae*

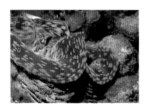

giant clam
Tridacna squamosa

purple-tip nudibranch
Janolus sp.

striped anemone
Rhodactis sp.

blue tunicate
Rhopalaea crassa

tunicate colony
Didemnum sp.

candelabra sponge
Haliclona fascigera

Hazardous Marine Life

Marine animals almost never attack divers, but many have defensive and offensive weaponry that can be triggered if they feel threatened or annoyed. The ability to recognize hazardous creatures is a valuable asset in avoiding accident and injury. The following are some of the potentially hazardous creatures most commonly found in Bali and Lombok.

Sharks

Sharks come in many shapes and sizes. They are most recognizable by their triangular dorsal fin. Though many species are shy, there are occasional attacks. About 25 species worldwide are considered dangerous to humans. Sharks will generally not attack unless provoked, so don't taunt, tease or feed them. Avoid spearfishing, carrying fish baits or mimicking a wounded fish and your likelihood of being attacked will greatly diminish. Face and quietly watch any shark that is acting aggressively and be prepared to push it away with camera, knife or tank. If someone is bitten by a shark, stop the bleeding, reassure the patient, treat for shock and seek immediate medical treatment.

Sea Snakes

Air-breathing reptiles with a venom that's 20 times stronger than any land snake's,

sea snakes release venom only when feeding or under extreme distress—so most defensive bites do not contain venom. Sea snakes rarely bite even if they are handled, but avoid touching them. To treat a sea snake bite, use a pressure bandage and immobilize the victim. Try to identify the snake, be prepared to administer CPR and seek urgent medical aid.

Lionfish

Also known as turkeyfish or fire-fish, these slow, graceful fish extend their feathery pectoral fins as they swim. Lionfish normally try to avoid divers, but will react defensively if threatened, accidentally bumped, stepped on or awakened. Lionfish inject venom through sharp dorsal spines that can penetrate booties, wetsuits and leather gloves. The wounds can be extremely painful. If you're stung, wash the wound and immerse in nonscalding hot water for 30 to 90 minutes.

Jellyfish

Jellyfish sting by releasing the stinging cells contained in their trailing tentacles. Stings are often irritating and not painful, but should be treated immediately with a decontaminant such as vinegar, rubbing alcohol, baking soda, papain or dilute household ammonia. Beware that some people may have a stronger reaction than others, in which case you should prepare to resuscitate and seek medical aid.

BOB HALSTEAD

Barracuda

Barracuda are identifiable by their long, silver, cylindrical bodies and razorlike teeth protruding from an underslung jaw. They swim alone or in small groups, continually opening and closing their mouths, an action that looks daunting, but actually assists their respiration. Though barracuda will hover near

divers to observe, they are really somewhat shy, though they may be attracted by shiny objects that resemble fishing lures. Irrigate a barracuda bite with fresh water and treat with antiseptics, anti-tetanus and antibiotics.

Scorpionfish

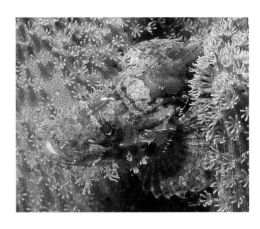

Scorpionfish are well-camouflaged creatures that have poisonous spines along their dorsal fins. They are often difficult to spot since they typically rest quietly on the bottom or on coral, looking more like rocks. Practice good buoyancy control and watch where you put your hands. Scorpionfish wounds can be excruciating. To treat a puncture, wash the wound and immerse in nonscalding hot water for 30 to 90 minutes.

Sea Urchins

Sea urchins tend to live in shallow areas near shore and come out of their shelters at night. They vary in coloration and size, with spines ranging from short and blunt to long and needle-sharp. The spines are the urchin's most dangerous weapon, easily able to penetrate neoprene wetsuits, booties and gloves. Treat minor punctures by extracting the spines and immersing in nonscalding hot water. More serious injuries require medical attention.

Diving Conservation & Awareness

On the whole, Bali and Lombok are beautiful islands to visit, but as in many places throughout the world, the marine environment is at risk. Visitors often complain about plastic bags and other trash they see floating in the water. Cyanide and dynamite fishing are common practices, as is shark finning, the inhumane practice of cutting off a shark's fin to sell to Asia's big-city restaurants. Obviously, monetary gain is often placed ahead of environmental concerns. This is a poor tradeoff, as economic analysis has shown that the value of tourism and sustainable fisheries resulting from intact coral reefs is 50 times greater than the value obtained through destructive fishing methods and reef mining. Education about conservation practices is one of the country's biggest challenges, and one of its greatest prospects.

Local conservation groups have sprung up to combat the current disregard of the marine environment and to promote a better understanding of the reefs and their delicate ecosystems. Villagers and fisherfolk are encouraged to make money by using, not abusing, their resources. Programs are being instituted to ensure that money from tourism also gets to grass-roots conservation efforts. International conservation groups are putting pressure on the Indonesian government to create and enforce environmental protection laws. The process of educating both locals and visitors, while creating a new philosophy of protecting the seas, is difficult, but worthwhile.

Marine Reserves & Regulations

Destructive fishing methods are illegal in Indonesia, and Bali has specific laws against the taking of endangered marine life such as sea turtles, dugongs and whale sharks. However, whaling ships are permitted to operate in Bali's coastal waters.

Bali and Lombok's two official marine reserves are Menjangan Island (an extension of western Bali's Taman Nasional Bali Barat) and the Gili Islands (off northwestern Lombok). Fishing is not allowed and divers may not take anything from the marine environment. A permit is necessary to dive around Menjangan—the operator you dive with will typically take care of this for you.

The marine reserves are, in theory, protected by law. Enforcement personnel are assigned to prevent fishing and to arrest gross violators like dynamiters and turtle-takers. Divers are rarely checked for shells and the like, as understaffed enforcement officials rely on the honor system and dive-guide surveillance.

Dynamite Fishing in Bali

Few regions have escaped Bali's biggest scourge to the reefs—dynamite (or blast) fishing. Homemade bombs—made of anything from petroleum products to fertilizer—are used in this destructive fishing method. The blasts cause fish to implode and either sink to the bottom or float to the surface. Though many of these fish are collected, a substantial number are left to rot. The explosions also kill invertebrates and other marine creatures, and destroy habitat by shattering the corals. Even when the reef appears unscathed, the blasts cause cracks that weaken and stress it. Because of damaged or destroyed habitat, reef populations rebound slowly or not at all.

Dynamite fishing is illegal and punishable by 10 years in prison—assuming the offender is caught and convicted. The truth of the matter is that even when offenders are caught, they are rarely sentenced. Conservation officers are few in number and rather low-paid, so bribery is not unheard of. As a result, there are many repeat offenders and the practice is still going full-force.

Dynamite fisherfolk generally won't blast if a dive boat is nearby and there's someone around to report them. However, it is not unusual for a sport diver to hear a blast while diving. The sound may seem terrifyingly loud even if the blast is far away because sound travels well underwater.

Dive operators do what they can to report known offenders, but corruption is a fact of life in these matters. Only continued pressure on Bali and Indonesia's lawmakers and enforcement divisions will put a stop to dynamite fishing.

Education is, of course, the key to getting people to understand the value of healthy reefs and the mass waste

Dynamite fishing can reduce a coral reef to rubble.

caused by dynamite fishing. Unfortunately, enlightenment may come too late, so enforcement is a necessary tool for Bali's diverse reefs to remain healthy.

In other popular diving areas, local dive operators and hotels have declared their areas marine parks or preserves. Dive-center staff members work with the neighboring villages to ensure the protection of the reefs and local marine life.

Responsible Diving

Dive sites tend to be located where the reefs and walls display the most beautiful corals and sponges. It only takes a moment—an inadvertently placed hand or knee, or a careless brush or kick with a fin—to destroy this fragile, living part of our delicate ecosystem. By following certain basic guidelines while diving, you can help preserve the ecology and beauty of the reefs:

1. Never drop boat anchors onto a coral reef and take care not to ground boats on coral. Encourage dive operators and regulatory bodies in their efforts to establish and use permanent moorings at appropriate dive sites.

2. Practice and maintain proper buoyancy control and avoid over-weighting. Be aware that buoyancy can change over the period of an extended trip. Initially you may breathe harder and need more weighting; a few days later you may breathe more easily and need less weight. Tip: Use your weight belt and tank position to maintain a horizontal position—raise them to elevate your feet, lower them to elevate your upper body. Also be careful about buoyancy loss: as you go deeper, your wetsuit compresses, as does the air in your BC.

3. Avoid touching living marine organisms with your body and equipment. Polyps can be damaged by even the gentlest contact. Never stand on or touch living coral. If you must hold on to the reef, touch only exposed rock or dead coral.

4. Take great care in underwater caves and inside shipwrecks. Spend as little time within them as possible, as your air bubbles can damage fragile organisms and increase oxidation. Divers should take turns inspecting the interiors of small caves or under ledges to lessen the chances of damaging contact.

5. Be conscious of your fins. Even without contact, the surge from heavy fin strokes near the reef can do damage. Avoid full-leg kicks when diving close to the bottom and when leaving a photo scene. When you inadvertently kick something, stop kicking! It seems obvious, but some divers either panic or are totally oblivious when they bump something. When treading water in shallow reef areas, take care not to kick up clouds of sand. Settling sand can smother the delicate reef organisms.

6. Secure gauges, computer consoles and the octopus regulator so they're not dangling—they are like miniature wrecking balls to a reef.

7. When swimming in strong currents, be extra careful about leg kicks and handholds.

8. Photographers should take extra precautions, as cameras and equipment affect buoyancy. Changing f-stops, framing a subject and maintaining position for a photo often conspire to prohibit the ideal "no-touch" approach on a reef. When you must use "holdfasts," choose them intelligently (i.e., use one finger only for leverage off an area of dead coral).

9. Resist the temptation to collect or buy coral or shells. Aside from the ecological damage, taking home marine souvenirs depletes the beauty of a site and spoils other divers' enjoyment.

10. Ensure that you take home all your trash and any litter you may find as well. Plastics in particular pose a serious threat to marine life.

11. Resist the temptation to feed fish. You may disturb their normal eating habits, encourage aggressive behavior or feed them food that is detrimental to their health.

12. Minimize your disturbance of marine animals. Don't ride on the backs of turtles or manta rays, as this can cause them great anxiety.

Indonesian Marine Conservation Organizations

Coral reefs and oceans are facing unprecedented environmental pressures. The following local nongovernmental organizations *(Lembaga Swadaya Masyarakat)* are actively involved in promoting responsible diving practices, publicizing environmental marine threats and lobbying for better policies.

Pusat Pendidikan Lingkungan Hidup (PPLH Bali)
Jalan Danau Tamblingan 148
Sanur, Bali
☎ (361) 281684 fax: (361) 287314
pplhbali@denpasar.wasantara.net.id

WWF Wallacea Bioregion
Jalan Hayam Wuruk 179
Denpasar, Bali
☎ (361) 247125 fax: (361) 236866
wwf-bali@denpasar.net.id

The Nature Conservancy (TNC Bali)
Jalan Pangembak #2
Sanur, Bali
☎ (361) 287272 fax: (361) 270737

Wahana Lingkungan Hidup (Walhi Bali)
Jalan Noja, Gang 37 #16
Denpasar, Bali
☎ (361) 249630

Yayasan Wisnu
Jalan Pengubengan 94
Kerobokan, Bali
☎/fax: (361) 735320
greenbali@denpasar.wasantara.net.id

Listings

Telephone Calls

To call Indonesia, dial the international access code of the country you are calling from (011 from the U.S.) + 62 (Indonesia's country code) + the city area code (in parentheses in these listings) + the five- to seven-digit local number.

Diving Services

There are countless diving services available throughout Indonesia. The following is a broad (but not exhaustive) list of well-established and reliable services available in Bali and Lombok. These dive shops typically offer a range of rental and retail gear, courses and boat dives. Many operators offer overnight trips (often called "dive safaris"), which include transportation, diving and accommodations. Tanks and weights should be part of your dive package. Most dive shops also offer certification and advanced training classes and will accept Open Water referrals from virtually any certification agency. Generally, dive shops will accept most major credit cards, but with a small surcharge. Ask before booking.

Though a few Bali-based dive boats offer live-aboard trips to more-distant Indonesian islands, at the time of writing, no live-aboards regularly visit Bali and Lombok's reefs.

Tips for Evaluating a Dive Operator

Bali's recent tourism boom and the popularity of diving here means there are many reputable dive operators. Unfortunately, some businesses are shoestring operations that view training and equipment maintenance as a secondary concern. It pays to shop around before booking a trip.

Ask the shop about what equipment they carry, the boat you will be diving from, the divemasters' background and training, insurance coverage and trip costs. Take a look on the internet, and ask other divers about their experiences with dive shops in Bali and Lombok. It shouldn't take long to find an operator that suits your diving interests and budget.

Bali

AquaMarine Diving – Bali
Jl. Raya Seminyak 14 #12, Kuta, Bali
☎ (361) 730107 fax: (361) 735368
aquamar@indosat.net.id
www.aquamarinediving.com
Sales: yes **Rentals:** yes
Trips: Throughout Bali
Courses: PADI Open Water to Divemaster,
Juniors, Bubblemakers. Courses available in
English, German, French, Spanish and
Japanese.

Aquapro Bali
Jl. Bypass Ngurah Rai 46, E Blanjong,
Sanur, Bali
☎ (361) 270791 fax: (361) 287065
aquapro@balidiving.com
www.balidiving.com & www.divingbali.com
Sales: yes **Rentals:** yes
Trips: Throughout Bali
Courses: PADI Discover Scuba, Open Water
to Instructor, plus PADI & DAN Specialty
Courses.

Bali Hai Diving Adventures
Offices of Bali Hai Cruises,
Benoa Harbor, Bali
☎ (361) 720331 fax: (361) 720334
☎/fax: (361) 724062
diverse@indosat.net.id
www.scubali.com.
Sales: yes **Rentals:** yes
Trips: Throughout Bali (specializing in Nusa
Lembongan) & Lombok's Gili Islands
Courses: PADI Open Water to Divemaster in
English, German, Japanese and Indonesian.

Bali Marine Sports (Bali Persona Bahari)
Jl. Bypass Ngurah Rai #490, Blanjong,
Sanur, Bali
☎ (361) 270386, 289308 fax: (361) 287872
bmsdive@indosat.net.id
www.indo.com/diving/bms
Sales: yes **Rentals:** yes
Trips: Throughout Bali
Courses: PADI Scuba Diver to Assistant
Instructor

Baruna Watersports
Jl. Bypass I Gusti Ngurah Rai #300B,
Tuban, Bali
☎ (361) 753820 fax: (361) 753809
baruna@denpasar.wasantara.net.id
www.baruna.com
Sales: no **Rentals:** yes
Trips: Throughout Indonesia
Courses: PADI Open Water to Divemaster

Crystal Divers
Jl. Duyung 25 (next to the Bali Hyatt Hotel),
Semawang, Sanur, Bali
☎ (811) 385693 ☎/fax: (361) 286737
bcrystal@dps.mega.net.id
www.crystal-divers.com
Sales: yes **Rentals:** yes
Trips: Throughout Bali
Courses: PADI Open Water to Divemaster
plus specialty courses in English and Scandi-
navian languages.

Dive & Dive's
Jl. Bypass I Gusti Ngurah Rai #27, Sanur, Bali
☎ (361) 288652, 285530 & 283474
fax: (361) 288892
divedive@indo.net.id
www.diveanddives.com
Sales: yes **Rentals:** yes
Trips: Throughout Bali
Courses: PADI Open Water to Divemaster

Dive Indonesia (Bali Surf 'n Dive Center)
7 Pantai Kuta, Kuta, Bali
☎ (361) 766888 & 764888
fax: (361) 755103
deepblue@idola.net.id
www.diveindonesia.com
Sales: yes **Rentals:** no
Trips: Throughout Indonesia
Courses: Available at Dive Indonesia –
Trawangan Island

Eco-Dive Bali
Jemeluk Beach, Amed, Abang,
Karangasem, Bali
☎ 206-650-9666 (U.S.)
info@ecodivebali.com
www.ecodivebali.com
Sales: yes **Rentals:** yes
Trips: Tulamben, Amed, Lipah Bay, Gili
Selang, Menjangan & special tours
Courses: PADI Open Water to Divemaster
and specialty courses.

ENA Dive Center & Water Sports
Jalan Tirta Ening #1, Sanur, Bali
☎ (361) 288829 fax: (361) 287945
toll-free ☎: (361) 281751
enadive@denpasar.wasantara.net.id
enadive.wasantara.net.id
Sales: yes **Rentals:** yes
Trips: Throughout Bali, Lombok and
Sumbawa
Courses: PADI Open Water to Divemaster

Bali (continued)

Geko Dive Bali
Jl. Silayukti, Padangbai, Karangasem, Bali
☎ (363) 41516 fax: (363) 41790
gekodive@indosat.net.id
www.gekodive.com
Sales: no **Rentals:** yes
Trips: Throughout Bali
Courses: PADI Open Water to Divemaster

Mimpi Resort Tulamben
Ds. Kubu, Karangasem, Bali
☎ (363) 21642 fax: (363) 21939
tulamben@mimpi.com
www.mimpi.com
Sales: no **Rentals:** yes
Trips: Menjangan, Tulamben, Amed & Nusa
Penida
Courses: PADI Open Water to Divemaster in
English, German, French and Japanese.

Mimpi Resort Menjangan
Ds. Pejarakan, Banyuwedang, Singaraja, Bali
☎ (82) 8362729 fax: (82) 8362728
mimpi@denpasar.nusantara.net.id
www.mimpi.com
Sales: yes **Rentals:** yes
Trips: Menjangan Island, Mimpi Bay &
Tulamben
Courses: PADI Open Water up to Dive-
master in English, German, Japanese and
Indonesian.

Pro Dive Bali
Kuta Center Block F, Shop #15, Jl. Kartika
Plaza, Kuta, Bali
☎ (361) 753951 fax: (361) 753952
info@prodivebali.com
www.prodivebali.com
Sales: yes **Rentals:** yes
Trips: Throughout Bali
Courses: PADI Discover Scuba, Open Water
to Assistant Instructor

Reef Seen Aquatics Dive Center
Desa Pemuteran, Gerokgak, Bali
☎/fax: (362) 92339
www.soneva-pavilion.com/ganesha
/diving.html
Sales: no **Rentals:** yes
Trips: Pemuteran & Menjangan Island
Courses: Subject to availability of instructor

Sanur Dive College
Jl. Bypass Ngurah Rai #215, Sanur, Bali
☎ (361) 284025, 284026
fax: (361) 284027
sanurdivecollege@eksadata.com
www.sanurdivecollege.com
Sales: yes **Rentals:** yes
Trips: Throughout Indonesia
Courses: Open Water to Assistant Instructor
and IDC

Tauch Terminal Bali
Jl. Br. Basangkasa 111, Kuta, Bali
☎ (361) 730200 & 730201
fax: (361) 774508 & 778141
dive@tauch-terminal.com
www.tauch-terminal.com
Sales: yes **Rentals:** yes
Trips: Throughout Bali & Lombok's Gili
Islands
Courses: Open Water to Instructor in
German, English, Spanish, French and
Indonesian.

Tauch Terminal Tulamben Resort
Jl. Raya, Tulamben, Karangasem, Kubu, Bali
☎ (363) 22911 fax: (361) 778141
resort@tauch-terminal.com
www.divebali.com
Sales: yes **Rentals:** yes
Trips: Bali's East Coast, Menjangan Island,
Nusa Penida & Nusa Lembongan
Courses: PADI Open Water to Instructor in
German, English and Indonesian. Spanish,
French and Danish are also spoken.

YOS Marine Adventures (3 locations)
Jl. Pratama 106X, Tanjung Benoa,
Nusa Dua, Bali
☎ (361) 773774, 775440, 752005
fax: (361) 752985
Pondok Sari Hotel, Pemuteran, Bali
☎/fax: (362) 92337
Hotel Indra, Udhayana, Amed, Bali
☎/fax: (363) 22349
info@yosdive.com
www.yosdive.com
Sales: yes (Tanjung Benoa only) **Rentals:** yes
Trips: Throughout Bali
Courses: PADI Open Water, Advanced Diver,
Rescue Diver and Divemaster